MW00909116

FANTASTIC FACTS ABOUT

BATTLES, WARS AND REVOLUTIONS

Author
Anita Ganeri, Hazel Mary Martell, Brian Williams

Editor
Jane Walker

Design
First Edition

Image Coordination
Ian Paulyn

Production Assistant
Rachel Jones

Index
Jane Parker

Editorial Director
Paula Borton

Design Director
Clare Sleven

Publishing Director
Jim Miles

This is a Parragon Publishing Book

This edition is published in 2001

Parragon Publishing, Queen Street House, 4 Queen Street, Bath BA1 1HE, UK

Copyright Parragon © 2000

Parragon has previously printed this material in 1999 as part of the Factfinder series

2 4 6 8 10 9 7 5 3 1

Produced by Miles Kelly Publishing Ltd
Bardfield Centre, Great Bardfield, Essex CM7 4SL

ISBN 0-75254-880-8

Printed in China

FANTASTIC FACTS ABOUT

BATTLES, WARS AND REVOLUTIONS

p

CONTENTS

INTRODUCTION

To a large extent, the history of civilization has been shaped by its battles and wars. Here you will encounter warriors and soldiers, kings and politicians through the ages. Find out about civil war in England and America, and about revolutions in China and France. Finally discover the impact of two world wars in the 20th century and how conflict around the globe has affected all our lives.

BATTLES, WARS, AND REVOLUTIONS is a handy reference guide in the *Fascinating Facts* series. Each book has been specially compiled with a collection of stunning illustrations and photographs which bring the subject to life. Hundreds of facts and figures are presented in a variety of interesting ways and time-bars provide information at-a-glance. This unique combination is fun and easy to use and makes learning a pleasure.

VIKING RAIDERS

From the late 700s, bands of Vikings sailed overseas in their longships, landing on the coasts of western Europe. They raided monasteries and towns, carrying off slaves and booty, and seized land. From 865 Vikings from Denmark settled in eastern England. They attacked what is now France, but were bought off with the gift of Normandy in 911. Norwegian Vikings settled in Iceland and Greenland, and landed in North America. Vikings wandered in the markets of Baghdad and Constantinople, bringing back exotic goods to towns such as Jorvik (York) and Dublin.

Viking warrior

Chain-mail tunic

Iron sword

Leather shield

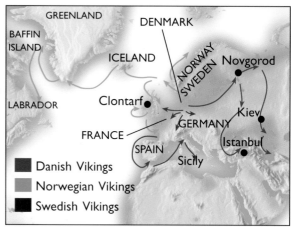

GREENLAND
DENMARK
BAFFIN ISLAND
ICELAND
NORWAY
SWEDEN
Novgorod
LABRADOR
Clontarf
Kiev
FRANCE
GERMANY
SPAIN
Istanbul
Sicily

- ■ Danish Vikings
- ■ Norwegian Vikings
- ■ Swedish Vikings

VIKING TRADE ROUTES
The Vikings traveled by sea and overland to England and Ireland in the west, and as far east as Baghdad and Istanbul.

VIKING INFLUENCE

Many Vikings were peaceful farmers and traders who chose to settle in the new lands, mingling with the local people. In England, King Alfred defeated the invaders, but Viking settlements in eastern England (the Danelaw) left a permanent legacy in customs, laws, place names, and language.

A VIKING RAID

The Vikings were fierce fighters with their favorite iron swords and axes. During an attack, raiders would rush from their longships. The ships could be rowed up rivers and land on beaches, so Vikings often took their enemies by surprise.

Iron ax

The heavy Viking sword was swung in a wide arc.

Oared longship

787 First reported Viking raids on English coast.

795 Vikings begin attacks on Ireland.

834 Vikings raid Dorestad (the Netherlands).

865 Great army of Vikings lands in England.

866 Vikings capture the city of York (Jorvik) in England.

878 English and Vikings agree to divide England between them after Vikings are defeated by King Alfred.

911 Vikings are given Normandy to prevent further attacks on France.

1016–1035 Reign of Canute, Viking king of England, Denmark, and Norway.

1066 Last big Viking attack on England, by Harold Hardrada of Norway.

MEDIEVAL CASTLES

Mighty stone castles dotted the landscape of Europe and the Middle East throughout the Middle Ages. The earliest castles were built by the Norman invaders of England. They were earth mounds, often built on hilltops, with a wooden stockade on top. The castles were soon enlarged and strengthened, with water-filled ditches or moats, stone walls protected by towers, and a massive central stronghold called a keep. Medieval castles were private fortresses for the king or lord who owned them. A castle was also a family home, although early castles were cold and drafty places.

CASTLE DEFENSES

The castle was defended by foot soldiers with spears and bows and by armored knights on horseback. When a castle was attacked, its walls had to be thick enough to withstand catapults, tunnels, and battering rams. The occupants often suffered from starvation or disease, and were forced to surrender.

FEASTING IN THE GREAT HALL
The lord and his followers feasted in the great hall. The lord and lady sat on a raised dais, and knights and other members of the household at lower tables.

Servants carried in food from the kitchen.

Musicians

Dancers entertained the feasting family.

Jousters

JOUSTING KNIGHTS
Jousting was combat on horseback between knights with blunt lances. It was a popular social occasion.

Dogs scavenged for scraps.

500 Byzantines build strong stone castles and walled cities.

800s Arabs build castles in the Middle East and North Africa.

1000s Normans develop the motte (mound) and bailey (enclosure) castle.

1078 William I begins building the Tower of London, England.

1100s Stone keeps become the main castle stronghold.

1180s Castles with square-walled towers are built.

1200s The concentric or ring-wall castle is developed.

1220s Castles with round-walled towers start to be built.

1280s Edward I of England orders a chain of great castles to be built in England and Wales.

1350s Castles made of brick are built in the Netherlands and England.

THE CRUSADES

For European Christians, the Crusades were holy wars, with the promise of plunder. For more than 200 years, Christian and Muslim armies fought for control of territory around Jerusalem known as the Holy Land. Jerusalem was a holy city to Jews, Muslims, and Christians but, in 1095, the Muslim Turks banned Christian pilgrims from the city. This angered both the western Christian Church in Rome and the eastern Christian Church in Constantinople. Christians were called upon to free Jerusalem and so launched the First Crusade, or war of the cross.

Steep ramparts

A Crusader knight

ATTACK!
Once Crusaders had conquered lands, they built strong castles to defend them.

Battering rams broke down walls.

A Muslim warrior

SUCCESS AND FAILURE

The Crusades inspired stories of bravery and honor. Crusaders had to be tough to endure difficult conditions on their journey. In 1099 the army of the First Crusade captured Jerusalem. Yet none of the later crusades matched this initial success, and the Crusaders failed to win back the Holy Land.

Giant catapults threw balls of flaming tar.

Boiling oil was poured on attackers.

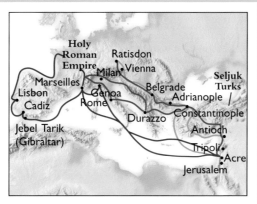

TO THE HOLY LAND
This map shows the different route to Jerusalem taken by the First Crusade (blue), the Second Crusade (yellow), and the Third Crusade (red).

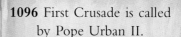

1096 First Crusade is called by Pope Urban II.

1099 The Crusaders defeat the Turks and capture Jerusalem.

1147 Second Crusade sets out.

1187 Muslim leader Saladin captures Jerusalem.

1189 Third Crusade is led by Frederick I Barbarossa of the Holy Roman Empire, Philip II of France, and Richard I of England.

1202 Fourth Crusade attacks Egypt.

1221 Fifth Crusade fights the Sultan of Egypt.

1228 The Sixth Crusade ends when Muslims hand over Jerusalem.

1244 Muslims retake Jerusalem.

1249 Seventh Crusade is led by King Louis IX of France.

1270 Eighth Crusade also led by Louis. He and many of his men die of plague in Tunis.

13

THE MONGOL EMPIRE

In the 1200s, Mongol armies sent a shockwave of fear around Asia and Europe, conquering a vast area of land that formed the largest empire in history.

The Mongols were nomads living on the plains of central Asia. In 1206, Chief Temujin brought all the tribes under his rule and was proclaimed Genghis Khan, meaning lord of all.

WANDERING NOMADS
The Mongols searched for fresh grassland for their herds, carrying their portable felt homes, called yurts, with them.

WARRIORS ON HORSEBACK
Mongol warriors fought on horseback. They controlled their horses with their feet, leaving their hands free to shoot bows and hurl spears.

Mongol soldiers were expert archers.

Spear

Bow

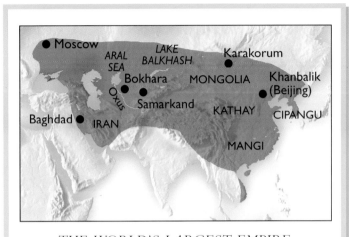

THE WORLD'S LARGEST EMPIRE
*Although ruthless in battle, Genghis Khan kept peace
in his empire. It stretched from the River Danube in
the west to the Pacific shores of Asia in the east.*

MONGOL CONQUESTS

The Mongols quickly conquered the Persian
Empire. They continued their attacks after
Genghis Khan died and, in 1237, a Mongol
army led by Batu Khan, one of Genghis's sons,
invaded Russia. Western Europe was saved only
when the Mongols turned homeward on the
death of Ogodai Khan in 1241. Enemies feared
the Mongols' speed and ferocity in battle. In
victory, the Mongols were usually merciless,
slaughtering people and plundering treasure.
Yet they ruled their empire fairly if sternly.

1206 Temujin becomes
chief of all the
Mongols, taking the
name Genghis Khan.

1215 Beijing, capital of
China, is taken by
the Mongols.

1217 The Mongols
control all China and
Korea.

1219 The Mongols attack
the empire of
Khwarezm (Persia
and Turkey).

1224 Mongol armies
invade Russia,
Poland, and Hungary.

1227 Genghis Khan dies.

1229 Genghis's son,
Ogodai, becomes
khan.

1237 Mongol army
known as the
Golden Horde
invades northern
Russia.

1241 Ogodai dies and
his armies pull back
from Europe.

15

KUBLAI KHAN AND CHINA

Kublai Khan, grandson of Genghis Khan, became leader of the Mongols in 1260. His armies moved from the windswept steppes of central Asia to overthrow the Song Dynasty in China, and by 1279 he controlled most of this vast country. At this time, China was the world's most sophisticated, technologically advanced country. The new Mongol emperor moved his capital to Beijing, taking care to maintain many aspects of Chinese culture. Chinese silks, porcelain, and other luxuries astonished travelers from Europe and Africa. After Kublai Khan's death, the Mongol Empire declined and had largely broken up by the mid-1300s.

ALONG THE SILK ROAD
Merchants traveled in caravans for protection against bandits. From China, they followed the Silk Road across mountains and deserts to the markets of the Middle East.

Camels laden with Chinese goods.

Travelers rested at caravanserai, or rest stations.

MARCO POLO (1256–1323)
The Italian explorer Marco Polo toured China in the service of Kublai Khan.

A SOPHISTICATED NATION

After visiting Kublai Khan's court, Marco Polo wrote in praise of Chinese cities, China's fine postal system, and its paper money. The Chinese had discovered technologies such as paper-making. Other inventions included the magnetic compass and exploding gunpowder rockets.

EARLY PAPER

The Chinese began making paper in about 105. They used hemp or tree bark for fiber. Later, they mashed rags or old rope into pulp.

Pulp was spread on mesh trays to dry into sheets.

1216 Kublai Khan is born.

1260 Kublai is elected Great Khan of the Mongols.

1271 Marco Polo sets out from Venice for China.

1274 Kublai Khan sends an army to invade Japan, but it is driven back by a storm.

1276 Mongols defeat the Song fleet near Guangzhou.

1279 Kublai Khan rules all China.

1294 Kublai Khan dies.

1368 Mongols are driven from China by Ming forces.

1395 Tamerlane, a descendant of Genghis Khan, invades large parts of southern Russia.

1398 Tamerlane invades Delhi, India.

1405 Tamerlane dies.

THE HUNDRED YEARS WAR

Edward III became king of England in 1327. He believed he also had a claim to the French throne so in 1337, he declared war on France. War between England and France lasted on and off until 1453. Edward's forces won a sea battle and two great land victories at Crécy and Poitiers, but were driven back by the French king Charles V. In 1360 Edward gave up his claim to the French throne in return for land.

Soldiers fought with a longbow, primitive cannon, and crossbow.

The English hoped Joan of Arc's death would end French resistance.

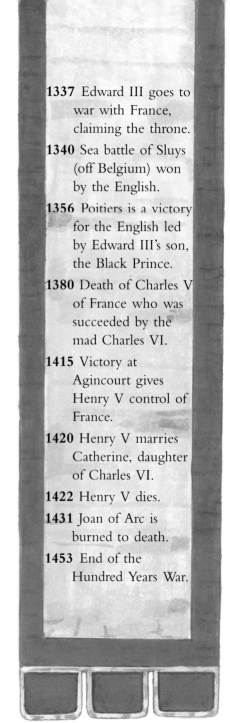

1337 Edward III goes to war with France, claiming the throne.

1340 Sea battle of Sluys (off Belgium) won by the English.

1356 Poitiers is a victory for the English led by Edward III's son, the Black Prince.

1380 Death of Charles V of France who was succeeded by the mad Charles VI.

1415 Victory at Agincourt gives Henry V control of France.

1420 Henry V marries Catherine, daughter of Charles VI.

1422 Henry V dies.

1431 Joan of Arc is burned to death.

1453 End of the Hundred Years War.

Years of truce followed until the English king Henry V renewed his claim to the throne in 1414. He led his troops to France, where they defeated a much larger French army at Agincourt in 1415. To make peace Henry then married the French king's daughter, but he died in 1422 before his baby son could become king of France. The fighting continued as the French were inspired by a peasant girl named Joan of Arc (1412-1431). She fought until the English caught her and burned her at the stake. Under the weak rule of Henry VI, the English lost ground and by 1453, they had lost all French territory except Calais.

EMPIRES OF THE SUN

Two civilizations reached their peak during the early 1500s—the Aztecs in Central America and the Incas in South America. The empires of both civilizations eventually fell to Spanish rule. The Aztecs were fierce warriors whose empire stretched across Mexico. They were skilled sculptors, poets, musicians, and engineers, but in 1521 they lost their empire to Spanish treasure-seekers.

THE END OF AN EMPIRE
The Spanish were vastly outnumbered in their battles with the Incas. But the Europeans had horses and guns, both new to the Incas. When the Inca ruler Atahualpa was killed, the leaderless Inca armies were quickly defeated.

Spanish soldier on horseback.

The Inca armies were weak after seven years of civil war.

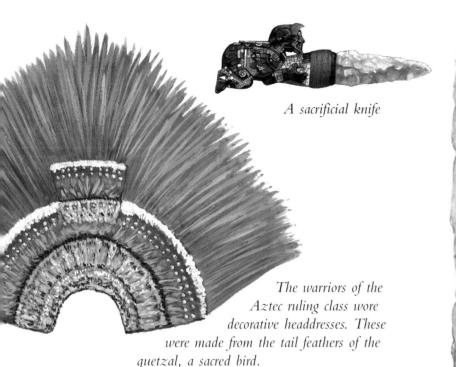

A sacrificial knife

The warriors of the Aztec ruling class wore decorative headdresses. These were made from the tail feathers of the quetzal, a sacred bird.

THE INCAS OF PERU

From the mountains of Peru, the god-emperor of the Incas ruled a highly organized empire. The Inca ruler Pachacuti and his successors increased the empire to include parts of Chile, Bolivia, and Ecuador. The Incas built stone cities, such as their capital at Cuzco, and fine roads for trade. In the 1530s a small Spanish expedition under Francisco Pizarro arrived to seek gold in South America. The Spanish killed the emperor Atahualpa and defeated his armies, causing the empire to fall.

1325 The Aztec capital of Tenochtitlan is founded.

1438 Inca Empire starts, under Pachacuti.

1440–1469 Reign of Montezuma I.

1450–1500 The Inca Empire is extended into modern-day Bolivia, Chile, Ecuador and Colombia.

1519 Hernando Cortés leads Spanish soldiers into Tenochtitlan. Montezuma welcomes them, believing Cortés is the god Quetzalcoatl.

1520 The Aztecs rise up against the Spanish. Montezuma dies.

1521 Cortés captures Tenochtitlan, ending the Aztec Empire.

1527 Death of the Inca emperor Huayna Capac; civil war starts between his sons.

1532 Francisco Pizarro, with 167 soldiers, attacks Inca forces and captures Cuzco.

21

MING CHINA

In 1368 a Buddhist monk named Ming Hong Wu founded the Ming Dynasty, which ruled China for almost 300 years. Under Hong Wu, China enjoyed peace and prosperity. He made Chinese society more equal by abolishing slavery, redistributing land, and demanding higher taxes from the rich. With a strong army, China reasserted its power over its neighbors. The Ming Dynasty was also a period of great artistic creativity.

JAPANESE INVADERS
Chinese soldiers fight against invading Japanese samurai. In the 1590s the Japanese tried to invade Korea, an ally of the Chinese.

Japanese samurai warrior

Chinese soldier on horseback

An arrow fired from a powerful bow could pierce a wooden shield.

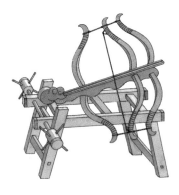

A CHINESE CROSSBOW
A powerful artillery crossbow like this could fire an arrow up to 650 feet (200 m).

CONTACT WITH OUTSIDERS

China's first contacts with European traders began in the 1500s, when Portuguese ships arrived. Western traders were eager to buy Chinese porcelain and silk and a new drink, tea, which first reached Europe in 1610. The Chinese had seldom looked far beyond their borders and after the mid-1500s the government banned voyages overseas.

THE FORBIDDEN CITY
From 1421, the Ming emperors lived inside the Forbidden City in Beijing, a huge complex of palaces, temples, and parks into which no foreigner was admitted.

1368 The Ming Dynasty is founded.

1398 Death of the first Ming emperor, Hong Wu.

1405–1433 Admiral Zheng He leads seven voyages to explore India and East Africa.

1421 The capital moves from Nanjing to Beijing.

1514 Portuguese traders arrive in China, followed by the Dutch in 1522.

1551 Chinese government bans voyages beyond Chinese waters.

1557 The Portuguese set up a trading base at Macao.

1560 Ming forces drive off Mongols and pirate raids, until peace and prosperity are restored.

1575 Spanish begin trade with China.

1592–1598 Ming armies help Koreans to fight off Japanese invaders.

1644 The last Ming emperor, Ssu Tsung, commits suicide.

TOKUGAWA JAPAN

The Tokugawa, or Edo, period brought a long period of stability and unity to Japan. In 1603 the emperor appointed Tokugawa Ieyasu to the position of shogun (a powerful military leader and effective ruler of Japan). Ieyasu, the first of the Tokugawa shoguns, ran the country on the emperor's behalf. His government centered on the fishing village of Edo, which later became known as Tokyo. Ieyasu reorganized Japan into regions called domains, each of which was led by a *daimyo* who controlled the local groups of warriors, or samurai.

SAMURAI WARRIORS
Boys trained from childhood to become warriors. Their main weapons were bows and arrows, single-edged swords, and daggers.

The Samurai fought on horseback as well as on foot.

Single-edged sword

Armor for protection

A WARLORD'S STRONGHOLD
Himeji castle was the stronghold of the warlord Hideyoshi during the civil wars that tore Japan apart.

JAPANESE ISOLATION

At first, Japan was visited by Portuguese, English, and Dutch traders. Missionaries converted many Japanese to Christianity. Ieyasu thought the new religion might undermine his rule and in 1637 missionaries were banned. Despite Japan's isolation from the rest of the world the country flourished and its population and food production increased.

A complicated hairstyle made it difficult to move the head.

JAPANESE SOCIETY
Under the strict society of the Tokugawas, wealthy women were treated as ornaments. The clothing and shoes they wore made it almost impossible to walk.

Long flowing gown

Very high shoes

1543 Birth of Tokugawa Ieyasu.

1560 Ieyasu returns to his own lands and allies himself with the warlord, Nobunaga.

1584 After several small battles, Ieyasu allies himself with the warlord Hideyoshi.

1598 After the death of Hideyoshi, Japan's warlords struggle for power.

1603 The emperor appoints Ieyasu shogun and the Tokugawa period begins.

1605 Ieyasu abdicates as shogun but continues to advise his successors.

1616 Death of Ieyasu.

1637 Christianity is banned in Japan and foreigners, except the Dutch, are forced to leave.

1830s Peasants and samurai rebel against the Tokugawas.

1867 The last Tokugawa shogun is overthrown.

25

THE THIRTY YEARS WAR

The Thirty Years War began in 1618 as a protest by the Protestant noblemen of Bohemia (now part of the Czech Republic) against their Catholic rulers, the Habsburg Holy Roman emperors. The war ended in 1648 with the Treaty of Westphalia, which gave religious freedom and independence to Protestant states. The long war devastated many states in Germany. Some lost more than half their population through disease, famine, and fighting.

SWEDEN AT WAR
Gustavus II Adolphus of Sweden led his troops against the Habsburgs because he believed the Protestant religion was being destroyed.

King Gustavus II Adolphus always fought at the head of his men.

A RELIGIOUS WAR

In 1619 Ferdinand II became Holy Roman emperor but rebellion against his rule soon spread to Germany. In 1620 Ferdinand defeated the Protestant king Frederick and soon Catholicism was the only religion allowed in Bohemia. Spain, also ruled by the Habsburgs, joined the war on the side of the Holy Roman Empire. Believing the Protestant religion to be in danger, the Swedish king Gustavus II Adolphus joined the war against Spain and the Holy Roman Empire. France, although Catholic, also entered the war in order to curtail Habsburg power.

BOHEMIAN PROTEST
The Thirty Years War began after a group of Bohemians threw two Catholics out of a castle window

1618 Thirty Years War starts.

1619 Ferdinand II is crowned Holy Roman emperor.

1620 Ferdinand's army defeats Protestant king Frederick of Bohemia.

1621 Fighting breaks out between Dutch and Spanish in the Rhineland.

1625 Denmark and England join in the war on the side of the Dutch.

1630 King Gustavus II Adolphus of Sweden joins the war on the Protestant side.

1635 Richelieu takes France into the war against the Habsburgs.

1637 French and allies start to defeat Spain.

1648 The Treaty of Westphalia brings an end to the Thirty Years War.

27

ENGLISH CIVIL WAR

The English Civil War broke out during the reign of Charles I. The king came into regular conflict with parliament, which he dissolved in 1629. For 11 years Charles ruled without parliament's help, but he later recalled it in order to raise money to fight a rebellion in Scotland. When the king tried to arrest five of his opponents in parliament in 1642, civil war broke out. At first the king's forces, or Royalists, were more successful than Parliament's supporters, the Roundheads. Eventually, in 1645, the Roundheads defeated Charles's forces. Charles was found guilty of treason and executed in 1649.

A Roundhead soldier

MAJOR BATTLES
This map shows the main battles of the war. After 1644, the king's forces, the Royalists, held the pink areas. Parliament's soldiers, the Roundheads, controlled the green areas.

Preston X X Marston Moor
Adwalton Moor X ● YORK

X Naseby

Worcester X X Edgehill
Cropredy Bridge X
● OXFORD
Bristol X X Brentford
Roundway Down X ● LONDON
X Newbury

Lostwithiel
X ● PLYMOUTH

Plain woolen jacket

A Royalist
soldier

*Puritans were strict
Protestants who
dressed simply and
disapproved of
theater and dancing.*

THE ENGLISH COMMONWEALTH

After Charles's death England became a
commonwealth (republic) ruled by parliament.
Later, Oliver Cromwell ruled as Lord Protector.
His successor, his son Richard, was removed
from office. In 1660 Charles I's son returned
from exile to reign as Charles II.

DEATH OF THE KING

*Charles I was found guilty of treason and executed in January
1649. The execution took place on a scaffold outside the
banqueting hall of Whitehall.*

Priest

Executioner

Charles I

1625 Charles I comes to
the throne.

1629 Parliament tries to
curb Charles's power
and is dismissed.

1639 Rebellion breaks out
in Scotland.

1641 Charles makes peace
with the Scots, but
rebellion breaks out in
Ireland.

1642 Civil war begins. The
first major battle takes
place at Edgehill,
Warwickshire.

1645 The New Model
Army, led by Sir
Thomas Fairfax and
Oliver Cromwell,
decisively defeats the
Royalists.

1648 Charles starts a second
civil war, but is quickly
defeated.

1649 Charles is executed on
January 31.

1653–1658 Oliver
Cromwell rules as Lord
Protector.

1660 Restoration of the
monarchy; Charles II
comes to the throne.

29

NAPOLEON

Napoleon Bonaparte made his name in the French army, rising to become the Emperor of France. He became an officer at the age of 16, and won his first victory against rebels during the French Revolution. In 1798 the French army, under Napoleon, defeated the Egyptians and the Ottomans, but the French navy was itself defeated by the British at the battle of the Nile. Napoleon overthrew the *Directoire*, or committee, that ruled France and in 1804 he proclaimed himself Emperor.

THE CODE NAPOLEON
Napoleon introduced a code of laws that incorporated many of the ideas of the French Revolution.

THE BATTLE OF AUSTERLITZ
In December 1805, a French army of 73,000, under the command of Napoleon and his generals, defeated an army of 87,000 Austrians and Russians. The enemy was lured into a valley where many were killed.

This map shows the French empire under Napoleon I and the dependent states that were virtually part of it. The main battles of the Napoleonic Wars are also shown

THE NAPOLEONIC WARS

Napoleon was a brilliant general who commanded thousands of conscripted men. In 1805 the British, under Lord Nelson, defeated the French fleet at Trafalgar. On land, Napoleon seemed undefeatable, but in 1812 his invasion of Russia was disastrous and his army in Spain suffered setbacks. After abdicating in 1814, he raised a new army the following year. Napoleon was defeated at the battle of Waterloo.

1769 Birth of Napoleon at Ajaccio, Corsica.

1795 Napoleon defends Paris against rebels.

1798 Nelson defeats the French fleet at the battle of the Nile, Egypt.

1802 Napoleon plans to invade Britain.

1803 Britain declares war on France.

1804 Napoleon declares himself emperor of France.

1805 Nelson defeats French fleet at Trafalgar. Napoleon defeats the Austrians and Russians at the battle of Austerlitz.

1812 Napoleon's army invades Russia but is defeated by the harsh climate.

1814 Napoleon is forced to abdicate and is exiled.

1815 Napoleon raises a new army. He is defeated at the battle of Waterloo.

1821 Napoleon dies in exile.

SOUTH AMERICA

In the early nineteenth century Spain and Portugal still ruled vast colonies in South America, but the colonists had begun to fight for their independence. The main struggle against Spanish rule was led by Simón Bolívar from Venezuela and José de San Martin from Argentina. San Martin gained freedom for his country in 1816, but Bolívar's fight was longer and more difficult. He joined a rebel army that captured Caracas, capital of Venezuela, in 1810, but was defeated by the Spanish. Bolívar became the army's leader but was defeated by the Spanish again.

THE BATTLE OF AYACHUCHO
At the battle of Ayachucho in 1824, Simón Bolívar's army defeated the Spanish. He had finally secured independence for Peru. Part of the newly liberated Peru became the republic of Bolivia, named for Bolívar.

JOSÉ DE SAN MARTIN
José de San Martin freed Argentina from Spanish rule. He then led his army over the Andes mountains to help the Chilean people gain their independence.

FREEDOM FROM SPANISH RULE

In 1819, Bolívar led his army over the Andes into Colombia and defeated the Spanish in a surprise attack. He later freed Venezuela, Ecuador, and Panama from Spanish rule, making them part of the Republic of Gran Colombia. Bolívar became president of the new state.

BOLIVIANS TODAY
Today, Bolivians wear dress that combines ancient patterns with Spanish influences.

1808 Independence struggles begin in South America.

1816 José de San Martin leads Argentina to independence from Spain.

1817 At the battle of Chacabuco in Chile, San Martin and Bernado O'Higgins are victorious over the Spanish.

1818 Chile becomes independent from Spain.

1819 Simón Bolívar defeats the Spanish at the battle of Boyoca. Colombia wins independence from Spain.

1821 Bolívar's victory over the Spanish at Carabobo ensures independence for Venezuela.

1822 Brazil wins independence from Portugal.

1824 Bolívar wins independence for Peru.

1825 Bolivia is named for Bolívar.

1828 Uruguay wins independence from Spain.

33

AMERICAN CIVIL WAR

In the United States, by the early nineteenth century, industry and trade had developed in the North. In the South, agriculture and slavery dominated. When Abraham Lincoln, who opposed slavery, was elected president, 11 southern states formed their own Confederacy. This marked the beginning of the Civil War.

ULYSSES S. GRANT
Grant commanded the Union armies and led them to victory.

THE BATTLE OF BULL RUN
The battle of Bull Run, Virginia, in 1861 was the first major battle of the Civil War. Confederate forces defeated the Union army.

Union soldiers wore blue uniforms.

Cannon mounted on wheels.

Confederate forces wore gray uniforms.

GENERAL ROBERT E. LEE
Although Lee's Confederate forces were defeated, he was an outstanding leader.

NORTH VERSUS SOUTH

The North had more soldiers and more money, and the industry to provide weapons. It controlled the navy and was able to blockade southern ports, preventing the South from exporting cotton and getting supplies from abroad. The South won the early battles of the war, but in 1863, the war turned in the North's favor when Unionist troops defeated Confederate forces at Gettysburg, Pennsylvania. Lincoln announced his aim to abolish slavery throughout the United States. By the time the Confederates surrendered in 1865, much of the South lay in ruins.

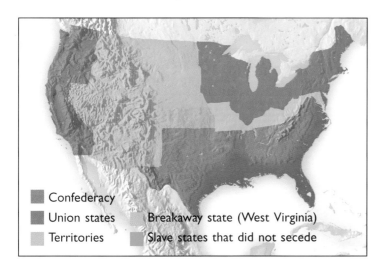

Confederacy
Union states
Territories
Breakaway state (West Virginia)
Slave states that did not secede

1861 Civil War starts when Confederate troops attack the Union garrison at Fort Sumter, South Carolina. Confederates win the battle of Bull Run, Virginia.

1862 Confederate general Lee prevents Union army taking Richmond, Virginia and defeats another Union army at Fredericksburg, Virginia.

1863 Emancipation Proclamation is signed. Lee is defeated at Gettysburg, Pennsylvania. Grant's Union army captures Vicksburg, Mississippi.

1864 Union forces besiege Confederates at Petersburg, Virginia.

1865 Grant's forces capture Richmond, Virginia. On April 9, Lee surrenders to Grant, bringing the war to an end. On April 15, President Lincoln is assassinated by Confederate sympathizer John Wilkes Booth.

WORLD WAR I

By the late 1800s, Germany had become a major industrial and military power and France and Britain in particular felt threatened by this. Germany formed the Triple Alliance with Austria–Hungary and Italy, while Britain, France, and Russia formed the Triple Entente. Both Britain and Germany enlarged their navies, and all Europe's armies were expanding. In 1914, the assassination by a Serbian citizen of Archduke Franz Ferdinand, heir to the Austro-Hungarian throne, sparked off the war.

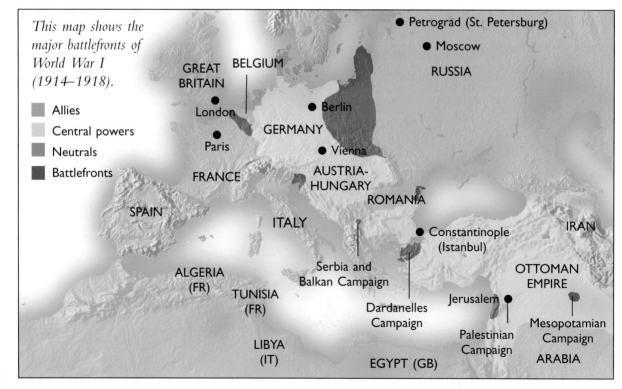

This map shows the major battlefronts of World War I (1914–1918).

- Allies
- Central powers
- Neutrals
- Battlefronts

Petrograd (St. Petersburg)
Moscow
RUSSIA
GREAT BRITAIN
BELGIUM
London
Berlin
GERMANY
Paris
Vienna
FRANCE
AUSTRIA-HUNGARY
ROMANIA
SPAIN
ITALY
Constantinople (Istanbul)
IRAN
ALGERIA (FR)
TUNISIA (FR)
Serbia and Balkan Campaign
OTTOMAN EMPIRE
Dardanelles Campaign
Jerusalem
LIBYA (IT)
Palestinian Campaign
Mesopotamian Campaign
EGYPT (GB)
ARABIA

THE FIRST TANKS
Making their first appearance in battle in 1916, tanks helped to break the stalemate of trench warfare.

THE GREAT WAR

Following the 1914 assassination, Austria–Hungary declared war on Serbia, and Russia mobilized its army to defend Serbia. Germany declared war on Russia and France. Britain joined the war to defend Belgium from German attack. The Great War involved two groups of countries —the Allies (France, Britain, Russia, Italy, Japan, and the United States) and the Central Powers (Germany, Austria–Hungary, and Turkey).

WAR LEADERS
The Allied war leaders led their countries to victory. The United States joined the war in April 1917.

David Lloyd George (Britain)   *Georges Clemenceau (France)*

Woodrow Wilson, President of the United States

1882 Germany, Austria–Hungary and Italy form the Triple Alliance to defend each other if there is a war.

1891 France and Russia agree that, if either is attacked, the other will give full military support.

1907 Russia joins with Britain and France to form the Triple Entente.

1914 June 28, Archduke Franz Ferdinand is assassinated by a Serbian protester in Sarajevo.

July 28 Austria declares war on Serbia.

August 1 Germany declares war on Russia to defend Austria.

August 3 Germany declares war on France, Russia's ally.

August 4 German armies march through Belgium to France. Britain declares war on Germany. World War I begins.

IN THE TRENCHES

Most of World War I was fought from two parallel lines of trenches separated by a short stretch of "no-man's land." This trench warfare was necessary because the power, speed and accuracy of the weapons used on both sides made it impossible to fight a battle in the open. When soldiers did go over the top of their trenches to launch an attack, often only a few yards of ground were gained and the cost in casualties was enormous.

LIFE IN THE TRENCHES

Soldiers slept and ate in their trenches, which were usually cold, muddy, and wet.

Life in the trenches was miserable.

Barbed wire helped to protect the trenches.

Dugouts (underground shelters) offered soldiers some protection from enemy shells and the rain.

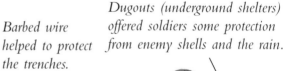

German Fokker
E1 monoplane

Sopwith Camel

WORLD WAR I PLANES
At first, planes spied on enemy trenches and troop
movements. Later, they were used in aerial combat and in
bombing raids.

THE ARMISTICE

In 1917, Russia started peace talks with
Germany. By September 1918 over 1,200,000
well-equipped US soldiers joined the Allied
forces. By October, almost all German-
occupied France and part of Belgium had been
reclaimed, and Turkey and Austria were
defeated. On November 11 Germany and the
Allies signed an armistice, ending World War I.

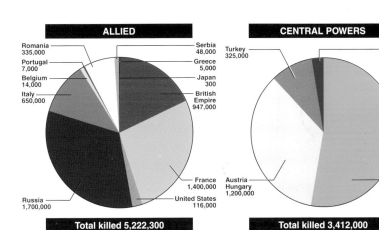

ALLIED

Romania 335,000
Portugal 7,000
Belgium 14,000
Italy 650,000
Russia 1,700,000

Serbia 48,000
Greece 5,000
Japan 300
British Empire 947,000
France 1,400,000
United States 116,000

Total killed 5,222,300

CENTRAL POWERS

Turkey 325,000
Austria Hungary 1,200,000

Bulgaria 87,000
Germany 1,800,000

Total killed 3,412,000

1915 British naval blockade of Germany leads to a German submarine blockade of Britain.

April–May Germany uses poison gas for first time.

1916 Battle for Verdun, France, lasts five months.

July 1 Start of the battle of the Somme.

1917 US joins the war on Allied side.

1918 March 3, Russia and Germany sign armistice.

July Germans launch offensive on the Western Front.

August Allies force Germans to retreat.

October Austria–Hungary surrenders.

November Armistice is signed on November 11 at 11 o'clock. World War I ends.

1919 Treaty of Versailles orders Germany to pay large amounts of compensation to its former enemies.

39

TROUBLE IN IRELAND

At the end of World War I, the question of Irish independence from Britain became critical. Most people in the six northern counties, known as Ulster, wanted to remain part of Britain, while in the south most wanted Ireland to become an independent republic. Conflict between the two sides pushed Ireland to the brink of civil war, only prevented by the outbreak of World War I. On Easter Monday, 1916, an armed rebellion declared Ireland a republic. After four days of fighting the protesters surrendered.

THE EASTER RISING
The Easter Rising of 1916 saw fighting on the streets of Dublin between British soldiers and Irish Republicans. Around 100 British soldiers and 450 Irish Republicans and civilians were killed.

Irish Republicans

British soldiers

Barricades were set up in the streets.

A DIVIDED LAND

After the 1923 settlement, three Ulster counties became part of the Irish Free State; the others remained in the United Kingdom.

THE REPUBLICAN STRUGGLE

In 1918, newly elected Sinn Fein MPs set up their own parliament in Dublin. The Anglo-Irish Treaty of 1921 made most of Ireland independent, leaving Northern Ireland under British rule. Civil war between supporters of the treaty and the Republicans ended when, in 1923, the Republicans accepted the division of Ireland for the time being.

EAMON DE VALERA
(1882–1975)

American-born Eamon de Valera took part in the Easter Rising of 1916. In 1932, his Fianna Fail political party won the Irish general election and he served as head of government for many years.

1886–1893 Attempts to give Ireland its own parliament are defeated.

1896 The Irish Socialist and Republican Party is founded.

1905 Sinn Fein, the Irish nationalist party, is founded.

1912 Outbreak of World War I prevents the enactment of the third Irish Home Rule bill.

1916 Irish Republicans in Dublin in armed revolt against British rule.

1918 Sinn Fein MPs set up their own parliament in Dublin.

1919 Outbreak of fighting between British troops and Irish Republicans.

1921 Anglo-Irish Treaty separates Ulster from the rest of Ireland.

1922 Outbreak of civil war between supporters of the Anglo-Irish Treaty and its opponents.

1937 The Irish Free State becomes Eire.

1949 Eire becomes the Republic of Ireland.

REVOLUTION IN CHINA

China became a republic in 1911 when the Kuomintang, the Chinese Nationalist Party, overthrew the Manchu Dynasty. When Chiang Kai-shek became Kuomintang leader in 1925, the Chinese Communist Party had already been founded. Civil war broke out between the two parties in 1927.

The Kuomintang claimed to govern the whole of China, but the Communists, under Mao Zedong, established a rival government in Jiangxi province. In 1933 Chiang Kai-shek attacked the Communists. In order to escape, Mao led 100,000 Communists on the "Long March." At its end he became Communist leader.

The Long March from Jiangxi to Shaanxi took 568 days and claimed around 80,000 lives.

About 100,000 marchers set off on the long journey.

The march covered about 6,000 miles.

Mao Zedong led the marchers.

COMMUNIST VICTORY

When the Japanese invaded China in 1937, the Kuomintang and the Communists united to defeat them. But in 1945 civil war broke out again. The Communists defeated the Kuomintang, forcing them off the Chinese mainland and onto the island of Taiwan. On October 1, 1949, mainland China became the People's Republic of China.

Mao Zedong
(1893–1976)

THE LONG MARCH
This map shows the route taken on the Long March from 1934 to 1935.

1905 Sun Yat-sen founds the Kuomintang (Chinese Nationalist Party).

1911 Collapse of the Manchu Empire. Sun Yat-sen becomes president.

1921 Foundation of the Chinese Communist party. Mao Zedong is one of its first members.

1925 Chiang Kai-shek succeeds Sun Yat-sen as leader of China.

1927 Start of civil war between the Communists and the Kuomintang.

1933 Chiang Kai-shek attacks the Communists in Jiangxi.

1934 Mao leads Communists on the "Long March."

1935 Mao becomes leader of the Communist Party.

1937–1945 The Kuomintang and Communists unite to fight against Japan.

1946 Civil war breaks out again.

1949 The People's Republic of China is proclaimed.

WORLD WAR II

World War II started on September 3, 1939, two days after Adolf Hitler's troops invaded Poland. The war was fought between the Axis powers (Germany, Italy, and Japan) and the Allies (Britain and the Commonwealth countries, France, the United States, the Soviet Union, and China). The Germans' tactics became known as the *Blitzkrieg* ("lightning war"). They made surprise tank attacks and overcame the opposition quickly. By June 1940, most of Europe had fallen.

AIR RAIDS
The bombing of cities and towns killed and injured many thousands of civilians on both sides.

THE BATTLE OF BRITAIN
The battle of Britain was fought in the skies above southeast England in 1940. Britain had far fewer planes than Germany but managed to win.

THE WAR CONTINUES

In 1940 Hitler's air force, the Luftwaffe, attacked southern England, trying to crush morale and destroy the British air force. The Germans were defeated, preventing Hitler's planned invasion of Britain. Hitler invaded his former ally, the Soviet Union, in June 1941. In December 1941, the United States joined the war following Japan's attack on Pearl Harbor in Hawaii.

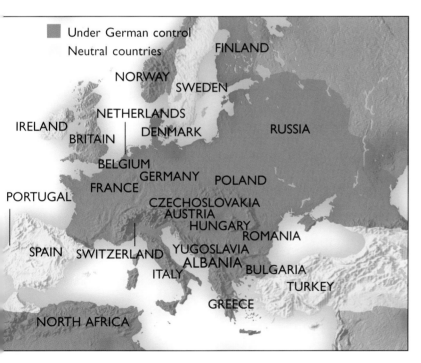

GERMAN CONTROL
By the end of 1941 the continent of Europe was almost completely under German control.

1939 Germany annexes Czechoslovakia. Italy annexes Albania. Italian/German alliance.

August 23 Germany and USSR sign non-aggression pact.

August 25 British, French and Polish alliance.

September 1 Germany invades Poland.

September 3 Britain and France declare war on Germany.

September 17 USSR invades Poland.

1940 March USSR takes Finland. German submarines attack British merchant ships.

April–May Germany occupies Norway, Denmark, Belgium, and the Netherlands.

June Germany occupies France. Allies evacuate from Dunkirk.

August–October Battle of Britain.

November Italy tries to invade Greece.

THE WORLD AT WAR

By May 1942 Japan had control of Southeast Asia as well as many Pacific islands. By August the US had defeated Japan's navy, stopping them from invading further territory. British troops led by Field-Marshall Montgomery won a decisive battle at El Alamein, Egypt, in 1942. The Allies in North Africa forced the Axis armies to surrender. German troops in the Soviet Union also faced great difficulties. In 1943 the Russians defeated the Germans at the battle of Stalingrad, with many lives lost on both sides.

WAR LEADERS
Montgomery defeated the Germans at El Alamein in 1942. De Gaulle was leader of the resistance movement in France. Roosevelt and Churchill met in 1943 to discuss the war's progress. The Japanese emperor's powers were diminished after Japan's defeat.

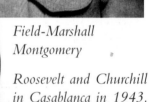

Field-Marshall Montgomery

Roosevelt and Churchill in Casablanca in 1943.

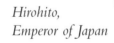

Hirohito, Emperor of Japan

Heinrich Himmler, head of the Nazi SS

THE ALLIED INVASION

By July 2, 1944 one million Allied troops had landed in France and were advancing toward Germany. In April 1945 they reached the Ruhr, center of German manufacturing and arms production. Hitler committed suicide in Berlin on April 30. Soviet troops captured Berlin, and on May 7 Germany surrendered.

Charles de Gaulle

THE SIEGE OF LENINGRAD
German and Finnish forces besieged the Soviet city of Leningrad from September 1941 to January 1944.

1941 February Allies capture 113,000 Italian soldiers in North Africa.

April Yugoslavia and Greece fall to Germany.

May German invasion of USSR begins.

December 7 Japan attacks Pearl Harbor. The United States declares war on Japan. Italy and Germany declare war on the United States.

December Japan invades Malaya and Hong Kong.

1942 February Singapore falls to the Japanese; 90,000 British and Commonwealth troops are taken prisoner.

May The Philippines and Burma fall to the Japanese.

August US victory at the battle of Guadalcanal ends Japanese expansion. The battle of Stalingrad begins.

October In North Africa, Allies defeat Axis forces at the battle of El Alamein, Egypt.

THE WAR ENDS

After the end of the war in Europe, fighting continued in Asia. In September 1944, US troops invaded the Philippines, while the British led a campaign to reconquer Burma. The US dropped an atomic bomb on Hiroshima, in Japan, on August 6, 1945. Three days later a second atomic bomb was dropped on Nagasaki. Thousands of people died, and many thousands more died later from radiation sickness, and other injuries. Five days later, the Japanese government surrendered and on August 14, World War II ended.

ATOMIC BLAST
The atomic bombs that were dropped on Nagasaki (above) and Hiroshima totally devastated the two cities.

D-DAY
The Allied invasion of Europe began on June 6, 1944 (known as D-Day). Around 156,000 troops were landed on the beaches of Normandy, in France, in the largest seaborne attack ever mounted.

Allied soldiers landed on five different beaches in Normandy.

The troops stormed ashore, often under heavy enemy fire.

Landing craft

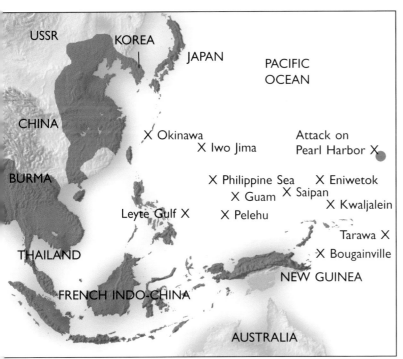

WAR IN THE PACIFIC
By 1942, Japan held all the orange areas on the map.
The crosses mark the ensuing battles in the Pacific.

WAR CASUALTIES

The loss of life from fighting was enormous, and others died through ill treatment as prisoners of war. Millions of civilians died through bombing raids or through illness and starvation. Around six million Jewish people died in concentration camps. After the war, leading Nazis were tried for war crimes and crimes against humanity.

1943 February The Germans are defeated at the battle of Stalingrad.

May Axis troops in North Africa surrender.

July Mussolini is overthrown and Italy declares war on Germany.

1944 June Allied forces land in Normandy, France.

October Allies invade Philippines.

December Start of battle of the Bulge, last German offensive.

1945 February Yalta Conference.

March US forces capture Iwo Jima.

April Hitler commits suicide.

May Soviet troops enter Berlin. Germany surrenders.

July Potsdam Conference agrees division of Germany.

August Japan surrenders after atomic bombs are dropped on Hiroshima and Nagasaki.

THE COLD WAR

Although the United States and the Soviet Union were allies in World War II, soon afterwards they became enemies in what was called the Cold War. The Soviet Union set up communist governments in Eastern Europe. To stop communism spreading to the West, the US-backed Marshall Plan gave money to countries whose economies had been ruined by the war. In 1948 the Soviets blockaded West Berlin (the city lay inside Soviet-controlled territory, but was divided between the Allies). The blockade was defeated, and the following year Germany was divided into West and East.

Symbol of the United Nations

A DIVIDED EUROPE
This map shows how Europe was divided after World War II. The boundary between the two halves of Europe was known as the "iron curtain." Few people crossed this divide.

NATO countries
Warsaw Pact
Neutral countries

FINLAND
NORWAY
SWEDEN
NETHERLANDS
DENMARK
RUSSIA
IRELAND
BRITAIN
EAST
BELGIUM GERMANY POLAND
LUXEMBOURG WEST
GERMANY CZECHOSLOVAKIA
FRANCE
AUSTRIA
HUNGARY
ROMANIA
PORTUGAL
YUGOSLAVIA
SPAIN SWITZERLAND
BULGARIA
ITALY ALBANIA
TURKEY
GREECE

NATO
In 1949 the countries of Western Europe and North America formed a military alliance known as the North Atlantic Treaty Organization (NATO).

Symbol of NATO

THE CUBAN CRISIS

Both the United States and the Soviet Union began stockpiling nuclear weapons. In 1962, the Soviet Union built missile bases in Cuba that threatened the United States. The US Navy blockaded Cuba and eventually the Soviets removed the missiles.

Soviet troops

Tanks blocked the streets of Prague.

THE INVASION OF PRAGUE
Soviet tanks entered Prague, Czechoslovakia's capital, in August 1968. A liberal government had introduced many reforms, which worried the Soviets.

1947 US-backed Marshall Plan gives financial aid to European countries.

1948 Blockade of West Berlin by the Soviet Union.

1949 NATO formed. The Soviets explode their first atomic warhead.

1955 Warsaw Pact formed among countries of Eastern Europe.

1956 Soviets invade Hungary to preserve communist rule.

1961 The Berlin Wall is built.

1962 Cuban missile crisis.

1963 The United States and Soviet Union sign Nuclear Test-Ban Treaty.

1964 The United States becomes involved in the Vietnam War.

1968 Soviet Union invades Czechoslovakia to preserve communist rule.

1979 Afghanistan is invaded by the Soviet Union.

1983 The United States invades Grenada.

THE VIETNAM WAR

Vietnam, Cambodia, and Laos made up the French colony of Indochina. During World War II Vietnam declared its independence. War broke out between the French and Vietnamese, ending in French defeat in 1954. Vietnam was divided into communist North and noncommunist South, but civil war broke out between the two countries. From 1959, communist guerrillas in the South, known as the Viet Cong, were helped by North Vietnam.

VILLAGE LIFE
Many Vietnamese civilians suffered greatly in the war as their crops and villages were destroyed to flush out and kill the Viet Cong soldiers.

SUPPLY ROUTE
The Viet Cong brought their supplies along the Ho Chi Minh trail, from China through Laos into South Vietnam.

HO CHI MINH (1892–1969)
Ho Chi Minh led Vietnam in its struggle for independence from France. Later, he fought for a united Vietnam.

JUNGLE WARFARE

The United States sent troops to help the South from 1965. In order to cut off supply lines, US planes bombed North Vietnam. Villages and jungle areas of South Vietnam were sprayed with chemicals to destroy Viet Cong hiding places. In 1969, after a Viet Cong offensive, the United States began to withdraw its troops. A cease-fire was agreed in 1973.

Most Vietnamese were farmers. They grew rice in the fields around their villages.

1946 Start of the war between Vietnamese nationalists and French colonial troops.

1954 Vietnamese communists defeat the French at Dien Bien Phu. The country is divided into North Vietnam and South Vietnam.

1963 South Vietnamese government is overthrown.

1964 War breaks out between North and South Vietnam.

1965 US troops arrive in South Vietnam.

1968 North Vietnamese and Viet Cong offensive.

1969 25,000 of 540,000 US troops are withdrawn.

1972 Peace talks start again.

1973 A cease-fire is agreed— US troops withdraw.

1975 The communists take control of Vietnam.

1976 Vietnam is reunited under a communist government.

MIDDLE EAST CRISIS

An uneasy peace followed Israel's defeat of the Arab League in 1948. Large numbers of Jews continued to migrate to Israel from overseas. The Palestinian Arabs began to campaign for a land of their own. In 1956 Britain and France fought Egypt over control of the Suez Canal. Israel felt threatened and invaded Egypt's Sinai Peninsula, destroying bases there. In the Six Day War in June 1967, Israel took control of all Jerusalem, the West Bank, the Golan Heights, the Gaza Strip, and Sinai. In 1973 Egyptian and Syrian forces attacked Israel but were defeated.

BEIRUT DESTROYED
Large parts of Beirut, the capital of Lebanon, were destroyed by fighting which began in 1976.

THE PEACE PROCESS
At peace talks in 1993, Israeli prime minister Yitzhak Rabin and Yasser Arafat, leader of the Palestinian Liberation Organization, guided by US President Clinton, agreed in principle to limited Palestinian self-rule.

President Clinton

Yasser Arafat

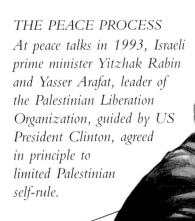

Yitzhak Rabin

AYATOLLAH KHOMEINI
(1900–1989)
Khomeini, a religious leader of Iran, came to power in 1979. He changed Iran into a strictly Muslim state.

WAR AND PEACE

In 1980 war broke out between the oil-producing countries of Iraq and Iran. In 1990 Iraqi troops invaded Kuwait but were defeated by UN forces. Peace agreements have been signed between Israel and Egypt, Jordan, and Syria, but tension and conflict continue to disrupt the peace process.

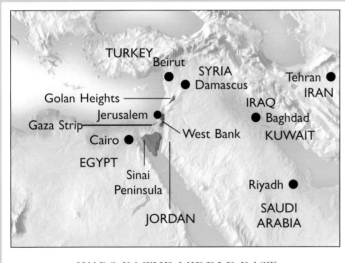

WARS IN THE MIDDLE EAST
The shaded area shows land taken by Israel in the 1967 Six Day War.

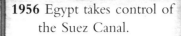

1956 Egypt takes control of the Suez Canal.

1964 Formation of the Palestinian Liberation Organization (PLO).

1967 Six Day War, between Israel and Egypt, Jordan and Syria, is won by Israel.

1973 Yom Kippur War between Israel and Egypt and Syria.

1976 Fighting breaks out in Lebanon.

1979 Peace treaty between Israel and Egypt. Islamic republican government is set up in Iran.

1980–1988 Iran–Iraq War.

1982 Israel invades Lebanon.

1990–1991 The Gulf War.

1993 Israeli and Palestinian peace talks.

1994 Israel and Jordan sign a peace agreement.

1995 Israel extends limited self-rule to the Palestinians.

THE COLD WAR FADES

In the early 1960s, the United States and the Soviet Union remained deeply suspicious of each other. Tension between them eased a little with the signing of two agreements to reduce the arms race. However, when Ronald Reagan, an extreme anti-communist, became US president in 1981, he increased military spending. In 1985 the new Soviet leader, Mikhail Gorbachev, introduced reforms, lessening tension between the superpowers. Two years later, Gorbachev and Reagan signed an agreement banning medium-range nuclear missiles.

CZECHS REVOLT
Czechoslovakians demonstrate in the capital Prague in 1989, demanding greater democracy without fear of recriminations.

THE COLLAPSE OF COMMUNISM

Gorbachev's reforms led to demands for free elections in Eastern Europe and by the end of 1989, communism had collapsed in Poland, Hungary, East Germany,

Demolishing the Berlin Wall

Czechoslovakia and Romania. In the following year, East and West Germany were reunited for the first time since 1945. In 1991 the Soviet Union was abolished, losing its superpower status. The Cold War had finally ended.

GORBACHEV'S REFORMS
Gorbachev opened the Soviet Union to Western enterprise, encouraging companies such as McDonald's to open up in his country.

1967 The United States, Britain, and the Soviet Union ban the use of nuclear weapons in outer space.

1972 The first Strategic Arms Limitation Talks (SALT) agreement is signed by the US and the Soviet Union.

1979 Second SALT agreement is signed.

1981 Reagan increases US military spending.

1985 Gorbachev makes reforms in the Soviet Union.

1989 Free elections held in Poland. Communism collapses in Hungary, East Germany, Czechoslovakia and Romania. The Berlin Wall is demolished.

1990 East and West Germany are reunited. Free elections are held in Bulgaria.

1991 Albania has a multiparty government. The Soviet Union is replaced by 15 independent nations.

57

IMPORTANT BATTLES OF HISTORY

Marathon (490 B.C.) The armies of Athens crushed an attempt by Persia to conquer Greece

Salamis (480 B.C.) Greek ships defeated a larger Persian fleet and thwarted an invasion

Syracuse (414–413 B.C.) During a long war between the city states of Athens and Sparta the Athenians besieged Syracuse but lost power after a heavy defeat

Gaugamela (331 B.C.) Alexander the Great of Macedonia defeated the Persians and conquered the Persian Empire

Metaurus (207 B.C.) A Roman army defeated a Carthaginian attempt to invade Italy

Actium (30 B.C.) A Roman fleet destroyed the Egyptian fleet of Mark Antony and Cleopatra, ending Egypt's threat to Rome

Teutoburg Forest (A.D. 9) German tribes led by Arminius ambushed and destroyed three Roman legions

Châlons (451) Roman legions and their Visigoth allies defeated the Huns, led by Attila

Poitiers (732) The Franks led by Charles Martel defeated a Muslim attempt to conquer western Europe

Hastings (1066) Duke William of Normandy defeated the Saxons under King Harold II and conquered England

Crécy (1346) Edward III of England defeated Philip VI of France, using archers to shoot his opponents

Agincourt (1415) Henry V of England defeated a much larger French army and captured Normandy

Orléans (1429) The French under Joan of Arc raised the siege of Orléans and began liberating France from England

Constantinople (1453) Ottoman Turks captured the city and ended the Byzantine (Eastern Roman) Empire

Lepanto (1571) A Christian fleet defeated a Turkish fleet in the Mediterranean and halted Muslim designs on Europe

Spanish Armada (1588) England fought off a Spanish attempt to invade and conquer it

Naseby (1645) Parliamentary forces defeated Charles I, leading to the end of the English Civil War

Blenheim (1704) During the War of the Spanish Succession, British and Austrian forces stopped a French and Bavarian attempt to capture Vienna

Poltava (1709) Peter the Great of Russia fought off an invasion by Charles XII of Sweden

Plassey (1757) An Anglo-Indian army defeated the Nawab of Bengal, beginning England's domination of India

Quebec (1759) British troops under James Wolfe defeated the French and secured Canada for Britain

Bunker Hill (1775) In the War of Independence, British troops drove the Americans from hills near Boston, Massachusetts

Brandywine Creek (1777) British troops forced American forces to retreat

Saratoga (1777) American troops surrounded a British army and forced it to surrender

Savannah (1778) Britain captured the port of Savannah from the Americans and gained control of Georgia

King's Mountain (1780) Americans surrounded and captured part of a British army

Yorktown (1781) A British army surrendered to a larger American force, ending the American War of Independence

The Nile (1798) A British fleet shattered a French fleet in Abu Kir Bay, ending Napoleon's attempt to conquer Egypt

Trafalgar (1805) A British fleet defeated a Franco-Spanish fleet, ending Napoleon's hopes of invading England

Austerlitz (1805) Napoleon I of France defeated a combined force of Austrian and Russian soldiers

Leipzig (1813) Austrian, Prussian, Russian and Swedish armies defeated Napoleon I, leading to his abdication the following year

Waterloo (1815) A British, Belgian, and Dutch army supported by the Prussians defeated Napoleon I, ending his brief return to power in France

Fort Sumter (1861) In the opening battle of the American Civil War, Confederate forces captured this fort in the harbor of Charleston, South Carolina

Merrimack and Monitor (1862) This inconclusive battle was the first between two ironclad warships

Gettysburg (1863) Union forces defeated the Confederates, marking a turning point in the American Civil War

Vicksburg (1863) After a long siege Union forces captured this key city on the Mississippi River

Chickamauga (1863) At this town in Georgia the Confederates won their last major battle

Chattanooga (1863) A few weeks after Chickamauga, Union forces won a decisive victory over the Confederates

Tsushima (1905) A Japanese fleet overwhelmed a Russian one, ending the Russo-Japanese War

Tannenberg (1914) At the start of World War I two Russian armies invaded East Prussia, but a German army under Paul von Hindenburg crushed them

Marne (1914) The French and British halted a German invasion of France at the start of World War I

1st Ypres (1914) A series of German attacks on this Belgian town were beaten back with heavy losses on each side

2nd Ypres (1915) The Germans attacked again with heavy shelling and chlorine gas, but gained only a little ground

Isonzo (1916–1917) This was a series of 11 inconclusive battles on the Italo-Austrian front

Verdun (1916) French forces under Philippe Pétain fought off a German attempt to take this strong point

Jutland (1916) This was the major naval battle of World War I; neither Germans nor British won

Brusilov Offensive (1916) A Russian attack led by General Alexei Brusilov nearly knocked Germany's Austrian allies out of the war

Somme (1916) A British and French attack was beaten back by German machine-gunners; total casualties for both sides were more than 1 million

3rd Ypres (1917) British and Canadian troops attacked to drive the Germans back, fighting in heavy rain and mud

Passchendaele (1917) This village was the furthest advance of 3rd Ypres; casualties of both sides totalled 500,000

4th Ypres (1918) This was part of a general German offensive, which died down after heavy fighting

Marne (1918) French, American, and British forces halted the last German attack of World War I

Britain (1940–1941) In World War II, German attempt to eliminate Britain's air force failed

The Atlantic (1940–1944) Germany narrowly lost the submarine war against Allied shipping

Pearl Harbor (1941) In a surprise air attack Japan knocked out the United States fleet at Hawaii

Coral Sea (1942) In the first all-air naval battle, Americans thwarted a Japanese attack on New Guinea

Stalingrad (1942–1943) The German siege of Stalingrad (now Volgograd, Russia) ended with the surrender of a German army of 100,000 men

El Alamein (1942) The British Eighth Army finally drove German and Italian forces out of Egypt

Midway (1942) An American fleet defeated a Japanese attempt to capture Midway Island in the Pacific

Normandy (1944) American and British troops landed in occupied France to begin the defeat of Germany; the largest ever seaborne attack

Leyte Gulf (1944) In the biggest naval battle of World War II, an American fleet thwarted a Japanese attempt to prevent the recapture of the Philippines

Ardennes Bulge (1944–1945) A final German attempt to counter the Allied invasion failed

Hiroshima/Nagasaki (1945) Two US atomic bombs on these cities knocked Japan out of World War II

Falklands (1982) A British seaborne assault recaptured the Falkland Islands following an Argentine invasion

Desert Storm (1991) An American, British, and Arab attack ended Iraq's invasion of Kuwait

INDEX

ACKNOWLEDGMENTS

The publishers wish to thank the following artists who have
contributed to this book.

Martin Camm, Richard Hook, Rob Jakeway, John James, Shane
Marsh, Roger Payne, Mark Peppé, Eric Rowe, Peter Sarson,
Roger Smith, Michael Welply, and Michael White.

All other photographs from the Miles Kelly Archive.

FANTASTIC FACTS ABOUT

SPACE EXPLORATION

Author
Tim Furniss

Editor
Steve Parker

Design
Pentacor

Image Coordination
Ian Paulyn

Production Assistant
Rachel Jones

Index
Jane Parker

Editorial Director
Paula Borton

Design Director
Clare Sleven

Publishing Director
Jim Miles

This is a Parragon Publishing Book

This edition is published in 2001

Parragon Publishing, Queen Street House, 4 Queen Street, Bath BA1 1HE, UK

Copyright Parragon © 2000

Parragon has previously printed this material in 1999 as part of the Factfinder series

2 4 6 8 10 9 7 5 3 1

Produced by Miles Kelly Publishing Ltd
Bardfield Centre, Great Bardfield, Essex CM7 4SL

ISBN 0-75255-605-3

Printed in China

FANTASTIC FACTS ABOUT

SPACE EXPLORATION

p

CONTENTS

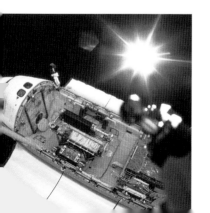

INTRODUCTION

For hundreds of years the only way of exploring space was by using a telescope. Today, with the astonishing advances of science and technology, spacecraft have explored almost every planet in our solar system, and humans have walked on the Moon. Find out about the rockets, stations, probes, and other objects we send into space, rapidly increasing our knowledge about the Universe as we begin the 21st century.

SPACE EXPLORATION is a handy reference guide in the *Fascinating Facts* series. Each book has been specially compiled with a collection of stunning illustrations and photographs which bring the subject to life. Hundreds of facts and figures are presented in a variety of interesting ways and fact-panels provide information at-a-glance. This unique combination is fun and easy to use and makes learning a pleasure.

SPACE EXPLORATION

Spacecrafts have now visited every planet in our Solar System, except the most distant planet, Pluto. Our exploration of space began when the first artificial satellite, *Sputnik 1*, circled the Earth in 1957. Within a few years, both the United States and the Soviet Union were sending rockets to the Moon to prepare the way for the first astronauts to land on its surface. Spacecrafts have been sent to explore the planets, some flying past their target or orbiting around it, while

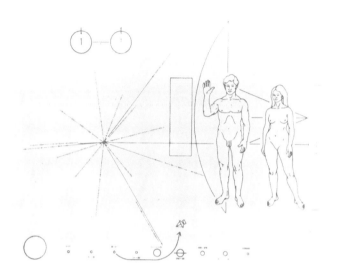

others land on the planet's surface. These spacecrafts send back valuable images and other data, allowing scientists to build up increasingly detailed information about our family of planets. Spacecrafts have investigated other objects in space too, including comets and the band of asteroids between Jupiter and Mars.

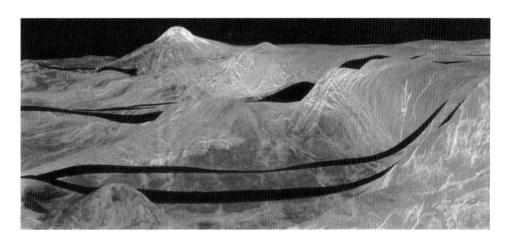

LIFTING OFF

For hundreds of years the only way to explore the planets was by using telescopes. All this changed in December 1962, when the American spacecraft *Mariner 2* flew past Venus. It sent back the first data about the planet, indicating that it was an extremely hot place. Since then, spacecrafts have explored every planet in our Solar System, except Pluto, and have also visited a comet and some asteroids.

Craft have landed on Venus and Mars, and have penetrated the swirling atmosphere of Jupiter. Other spacecrafts have orbited Venus, Mars, and Jupiter, while several planets have received fleeting visits from passing spacecrafts. Closer to the Earth, the first rocket was launched to the Moon in 1958, and since then 12 men have walked on the Earth's nearest neighbor. Spacecrafts have also explored the Sun closely. Through space technology our knowledge of the Solar System has reached new and very exciting limits.

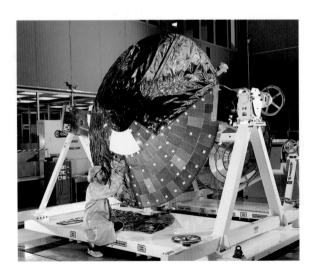

A VISITOR TO SATURN
The US/European Cassini–Huygens *spacecraft took 10 years to build. It is now on its way for a rendezvous with the planet Saturn in July 2004.* Cassini *will orbit Saturn while the* Huygens *probe will land on its moon, Titan.*

FIRST LANDING ON MARS

A Titan III-E Centaur D1 booster rocket launched the Viking 1 *spacecraft on August 20, 1975. The NASA spacecraft made the first soft landing on Mars.*

ANOTHER WORLD

The *Huygens* probe is expected to reveal Titan's surface as a world of methane seas, methane icebergs, methane snow, and a mixture of ice and rock. It will be dark, because the sunlight that filters through the orangy clouds gives a similar light to the light provided on Earth by a Full Moon. The main gas in Titan's atmosphere is nitrogen, and some scientists think that the orangy clouds may contain some organic material. This material is similar to that which has been created by scientists who are trying to simulate the formation of life on Earth.

LANDING ON TITAN

The European Space Agency's probe Huygens *should touch down on Saturn's moon, Titan, in November 2004. If this happens, it will be the first landing on the moon of a planet other than the Earth.*

11

EXPLORING THE SUN

The Sun has come under detailed scrutiny by a whole fleet of spacecraft since 1959, when the *Pioneer 4* spacecraft entered solar orbit after missing the Moon. Scientists were particularly interested in the particles of solar energy which affect the Earth and its upper atmosphere. They also wanted to try and understand how the Sun actually works. In 1962, the United States launched missions of Earth-orbiting solar observatories, called OSO. Later, two Helios spacecrafts and several other Pioneer spacecrafts were sent to operate in orbit around the Sun.

Special instruments on board the space station *Skylab* in 1973 and 1974 took images of the Sun in different wavelengths.

They revealed activity within the Sun's atmosphere that cannot be seen in visible light. *Skylab* carried its own solar telescope mounted on the outside of the station. More recently, the European Solar and Heliospheric Observatory (SOHO) was launched to conduct non-stop observations of the Sun, rather like a solar weather station.

SOHO OBSERVATORY
The European Solar and Heliospheric Observatory (SOHO) was launched in 1995. It will conduct the most comprehensive observation so far of the Sun and its radiation.

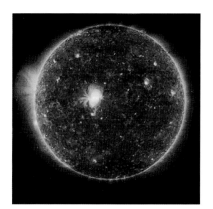

3.6 million degrees
Fahrenheit
(2 million degrees Celsius)

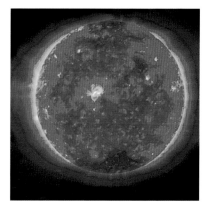

2.7 degrees million
Fahrenheit
(1.5 million degrees Celsius)

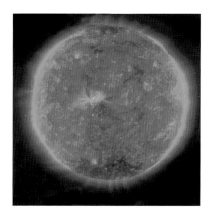

1.8 million degrees
Fahrenheit
(1 million degrees Celsius)

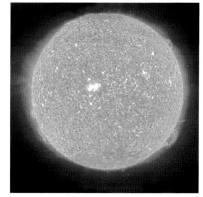

144,000 degrees
Fahrenheit
(80,000 degrees Celsius)

SURVEYING THE SUN

SOHO was placed into a special orbit 900 million miles (1.5 billion km) from the Earth. This orbit gives SOHO an uninterrupted view of the Sun from a point in space where the forces of gravity from the Sun and the Earth are equal. SOHO is part of an international program involving satellites from many countries. Their intensive survey of the Sun and its effect on the Earth is called the Solar Terrestrial Science Program.

IMAGES FROM SOHO
These ultraviolet images from SOHO show the different temperatures in the Sun's atmosphere. SOHO studied the Sun's surface activity, atmosphere, and radiation, including the solar wind. The study was made from a unique orbit that provided an uninterrupted view of the Sun.

VISITING MERCURY

It is almost impossible to view Mercury's surface with a telescope. In fact, until 1973 almost the only thing we knew about the closest planet to the Sun was that it must be very hot! The first, and so far the only, spacecraft to visit Mercury is *Mariner 10,* which was launched on November 3, 1973. Its flight path took it to Mercury using a fly-by of Venus. The spacecraft used the gravitational force of Venus as a "sling shot" to divert it onto the right course.

Mariner 10 made three separate fly-bys of Mercury, coming to within 3,576 miles (5,768 km) of the planet on March 29, 1974, within 436 miles (703 km) on September 21, 1974, and within 29,803 miles (48,069 km) on March 16, 1975. The images from the spacecraft were astonishing. Mercury is just like the Moon! It has thousands of craters, including a huge meteorite crater called the Caloris Basin.

VIEW FROM MARINER 10
Mariner 10 *gave us the first and only clear view of Mercury, showing it to be surprisingly like our Moon.*

MARINER 10 MISSION

Mariner 10 was a cut-price spacecraft flying a cut-price mission! To save money it was launched by a less powerful booster rocket, and as a result it needed to use Venus as a "sling shot". This meant that *Mariner 10* had to pass within a 240–mile (400–km) target area about 3,000 miles (5,000 km) from Venus, or else it would miss the opportunity to visit Mercury. To do this, the spacecraft had to fire its own engine very accurately several times during its journey.

FLYING PAST MERCURY

Mariner 10 *was launched in 1975. It was the first spacecraft to be sent to explore two planets in a single mission. It flew past Venus once and past Mercury three times.*

15

VENUS UNVEILED

Venus is a hostile planet and has posed a great challenge to space engineers. They have nonetheless succeeded in mapping almost the whole planet and have even landed crafts on its surface. Venus is surrounded by thick clouds of carbon dioxide gas that create a surface temperature of about 830 degrees Fahrenheit (460 degrees C).

The planet has an atmospheric pressure 90 times that of the Earth. It was first explored successfully by *Mariner 2* in 1962. The Soviet craft *Venera 4* penetrated the clouds, sending back some data in 1967, and in 1970 *Venera 7*'s capsule reached the surface still intact. *Veneras 9* and *10* became the first Venus orbiters in 1975, and their landing capsules sent

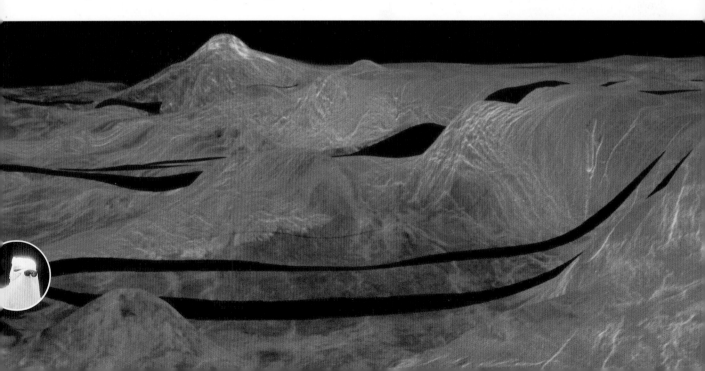

FLYING PAST VENUS
The first successful explorer of our
Solar System was the 446-pound
(203-kg) Mariner 2 spacecraft. It flew
past Venus at a distance of 21,080
miles (34,000 km) on December 14,
1962.

LANDING ON VENUS

The earlier Venera probes
proved that these spacecrafts
did not need parachutes to
complete their landing on
Venus's surface because its
atmosphere is so dense.
Veneras 9 and 10 landed at a
speed of 26 feet per second.
They were protected by an
ingenious shock–absorbing
system, rather like a lifebelt.
The capsule sat in the center
of a ring that was inflated
with gas before the landing.
An airbraking disk on top
of the capsule also served as
the radio transmitter.

back the first pictures of the surface — an
extraordinary feat in view of the harsh conditions.
Further Venera probes included those that sent
back some radar images that penetrated the thick
cloud. More recently, the *Magellan* Venus orbiter
was deployed from the space shuttle in 1989.

IMAGES FROM MAGELLAN
The Magellan *radar mapping satellite generated
false-color images of what the surface of Venus
looked like beneath the thick clouds.*

THE EARTH FROM SPACE

 The first astronauts to travel to the Moon were also the first to see the Earth as it might appear to explorers from another planet. On seeing the Earth as a tiny part of an enormous Universe, the *Apollo 8* astronaut James Lovell described our planet as a "grand oasis in the vastness of space". The *Apollo 8* crew's famous picture of the Earth as seen from space seemed to sum up Lovell's feelings.

After traveling into space to explore the Moon, the Apollo crew came back with something much more precious for the world's population — an appreciation of our tiny Earth as a fragile planet. As a result, there was an enormous increase in people's concern for the Earth's environment. People were also struck by the lack of real boundaries on the Earth's surface, unlike the view of the Earth that we see in a geography atlas.

THE RISING EARTH
In this picture taken during the Apollo 11 *mission the Earth seems to be rising above the surface of the Moon. The astronauts actually saw the Earth coming into sight around the side of the Moon.*

OUR BEAUTIFUL EARTH

For any astronaut, a view of the Earth from space is a captivating sight. Photos can never fully reveal the Earth's beauty and color.

A FAMOUS PHOTO

Many later Apollo crews took different pictures of the Earth from space, some of which show it as a fine crescent in the dark sky. The famous *Apollo 8* photo of the Earth rising was used on a US stamp. Each crew member — Frank Borman, James Lovell and Bill Anders — claims that he took the picture, jokingly repeating the claim whenever the three meet at public events. Anders was the chief photographer on board *Apollo 8* and he took the picture — but not before he was "ordered" to by Borman and Lovell, after protesting that it wasn't on his photo schedule!

VIEW OF THE WORLD

This classic view of the Earth was taken by the Apollo 17 *crew on their way to the Moon in December 1972. It clearly shows the land masses of Africa and Saudi Arabia, with the continent of Antarctica below.*

19

PROBES TO THE MOON

 Soon after the first satellites were launched into orbit above the Earth, the next obvious target in space was the Moon. The first attempts to send probes to the Moon were made in 1958, but the first object to hit the Moon's surface was the Soviet *Luna 2* spacecraft in September 1959. Later, *Luna 3* flew round the far side of the Moon, revealing what it looked like for the first time. Ranger probes took close-up photos before they crashed onto the surface in 1964 and 1965.

The first soft landings on the Moon were made by Luna and Surveyor craft in 1966. The unmanned *Luna 16* brought back samples from the Moon in 1970, the year in which the Soviet Union also launched an unmanned lunar rover called Lunakhod. After the first astronauts landed on the Moon in 1969, unmanned flights became rarer. *Luna 24* made the final flight of this era in 1976.

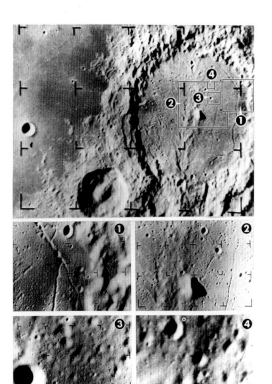

DESCENT TO THE MOON
These photos were taken on March 24, 1965 by the US spacecraft Ranger 9. *It was plunging toward the inside of the Alphonsus crater on the near side of the Moon.*

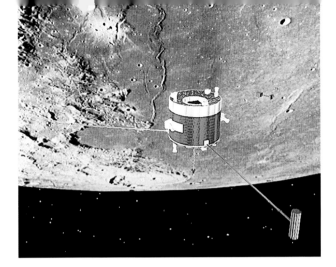

LUNAR PROSPECTOR

Launched in January 1998, Lunar Prospector *carried out a detailed chemical analysis of the Moon. The results confirmed that there might be frozen water under the bedrock in the polar regions.*

New interest in unmanned exploration of the Moon began when the US spacecraft *Clementine* was launched in 1994. It sent back data indicating that there may be frozen water under the rock around the Moon's poles. In 1998, NASA's *Lunar Prospector* began orbiting the poles and seemed to confirm this information. The water exists as ice crystals in the soil. If Moon bases are built at some time in the future, a water-extraction plant on the Moon would be needed to make use of this resource.

SURVEYING THE MOON

The US Surveyor spacecraft made the first rocket-assisted touchdowns on the lunar surface in 1966 and 1967. Some of the Surveyor craft carried robot arms fitted with scoops to collect soil samples.

21

MISSIONS TO MARS

 Mars has always held a particular fascination for the human mind because it is linked with the possibility that life may have existed on the planet at some time. The first Mars probe was launched in November 1960 but failed. This Soviet attempt was followed by many more, which, apart from *Mars 5* in 1974, all failed. In contrast to the failure of the Soviet missions to Mars, American spacecrafts to the planet met with spectacular successes. The first was *Mariner 4,* which took the first close-up images in 1965. *Mariner 9* went into orbit around Mars in 1971, and two Viking landers scooped up soil and took pictures in 1976.

In 1997 the *Pathfinder* spacecraft captured the world's imagination when it landed its *Sojourner* rover vehicle on the surface of Mars. The main quest now is to bring samples of Martian soil back to Earth. This task may be achieved by about 2007, after a series of lander–rover–orbiter and ascent vehicle missions that are due to start in 2003.

VIKING SPACECRAFT ON MARS
The first soft landings on the planet Mars were made by the American Viking 1 *and* 2 *spacecraft. They sent back the first photos of the Martian surface in 1976.*

IS THERE WATER ON MARS?

The Mars Climate Orbiter will enter polar orbit around Mars in September 1999. It will also act as a data relay satellite for the Mars Polar Lander, which is due to land on the edge of the largely frozen carbon dioxide polar cap about 600 miles (1,000 km) from the planet's south pole. A robotic arm will scoop up soil and deliver it to an on-board analyser. Scientists hope to find some evidence of the water that probably flowed across the Martian surface many years ago.

PATHFINDER TO MARS
After the Viking missions of 1976, the next soft landing on Mars was made 21 years later by the Pathfinder *spacecraft (far left). It carried a tiny roving vehicle called* Sojourner *(near left).*

LATEST VISITORS TO MARS
The next assault on the Red Planet got under way in December 1998 with the launch of the Mars Climate Orbiter *(top). This was followed by the* Mars Polar Lander *(bottom), which was launched in January 1999.*

FLYING PAST JUPITER

 Four spacecrafts have explored Jupiter, the giant planet of the Solar System. The first was *Pioneer 10,* which was launched in March 1972 and flew past Jupiter at a distance of 80,600 miles (130,000 km) on December 5, 1973. One of its most spectacular images was a close-up of the Great Red Spot. *Pioneer 11* followed on December 3, 1974 at a closer distance of 26,000 miles (42,000 km). It used Jupiter's gravity to sling it onto a course to make a rendezvous with the planet Saturn. The next visitor to Jupiter was *Voyager 1,* which was launched in September 1997 and flew past the planet at a distance of 173,600 miles (280,000 km) on March 5, 1979. It was followed closely by *Voyager 2,* which was launched first but arrived on July 9, 1979, at the closest-ever distance of 400,000 miles (645,000 km). Jupiter's most recent visitor is the *Galileo* spacecraft.

IMAGES FROM VOYAGER
Two Voyager spacecrafts flew past Jupiter in 1979. They returned spectacular pictures of the giant planet and its many moons.

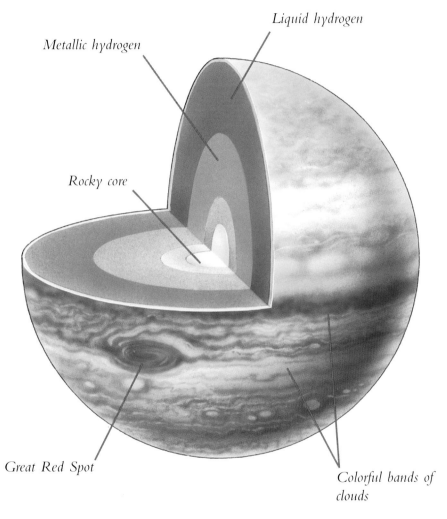

Metallic hydrogen

Liquid hydrogen

Rocky core

Great Red Spot

Colorful bands of
clouds

INSIDE JUPITER

Most of Jupiter is made up of gases, mainly hydrogen and helium. The swirling clouds are divided into a series of bands of different colors, mostly white, brown, and orange. Inside the clouds are crystals of frozen ammonia and frozen water, and molecules of carbon, sulfur and phosphorus. Below the cloud level is a huge sea of liquid hydrogen, and then a layer of metallic hydrogen. Here the pressure on the hydrogen is so great that it starts to behave like a liquid metal. Electricity flows through the metallic hydrogen and creates a strong magnetic field around the planet. At the center of Jupiter is a solid core of rocky material — it is about 20 times more massive than the Earth.

BEYOND THE CLOUDS
Thick clouds swirl around Jupiter, hiding the planet's surface from view. The different bands of color in the clouds are known as belts (the dark bands) and zones (the light-colored areas between belts).

INTO THE UNKNOWN

 The space probe *Galileo* was deployed from the space shuttle in October 1989. It became the first Jupiter orbiter in December 1995. The probe entered Jupiter's atmosphere of thick cloud, plunging into the swirling unknown at a speed of 30 miles (47 km) per second. *Galileo* sent back data for a total of 57 minutes, reaching a distance of 98 miles (157 km) inside the clouds. It was finally defeated by very high temperatures and by an atmospheric pressure 22 times higher than the Earth's. Scientists were disappointed with the data from the probe. There seems to be just one layer of cloud, with wind speeds of 2,110 feet (643 m) per second caused by Jupiter's internal heat.

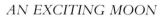

AN EXCITING MOON
One of the most exciting moons orbiting Jupiter is Europa. It may consist of an ocean of liquid water beneath a thin ice cap marked with thousands of cracks hundreds of miles long.

INTO JUPITER'S ATMOSPHERE
The first, and so far the only, craft to enter
Jupiter's atmosphere is the Galileo *capsule.*
It plunged into the tops of the planet's dense
clouds on December 7, 1995.

THE GREAT RED SPOT

Jupiter's Great Red Spot was first noticed by an English astronomer, Robert Hooke, in 1664. The oval-shaped spot is 31,000 miles (50,000 km) long and about one-third as wide. It is big enough to swallow up four whole Earths. The Great Red Spot varies in intensity and color. For example, it has recently been measured as only 24,000 miles (40,000 km) long. It is a huge whirlpool of storm winds situated in the planet's southern hemisphere. The red color indicates that it contains a lot of phosphorus, which has been carried upward from the planet's interior. The Great Red Spot slowly changes its position from one year to the next. It can be observed through an ordinary telescope.

VISITORS TO SATURN

 The first spacecraft to visit Saturn was *Pioneer 11*, which flew on to the ringed planet after its rendezvous with Jupiter. It passed the planet at a distance of 13,000 miles (21,000 km) on September 1, 1979. The first discovery it made was that Saturn's ring system does not consist of four divisions as seen in telescopes but of thousands of individual ringlets. Next, *Voyager 1,* which arrived on November 12, 1980 passing at a distance of 76,900 miles (124,000 km), followed by *Voyager 2* passing by at 62,600 miles (101,000 km) on 26 August 1981. The images returned from these crafts revealed Saturn's spectacular ring system in all its glory, as well as many of the planet's

CASSINI ORBITER
NASA's Cassini *spacecraft will deliver the* Huygens *probe into the atmosphere of* Titan. *It will then orbit Saturn and relay data from the probe back to Earth.*

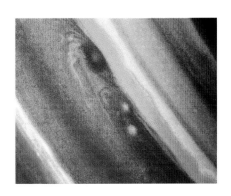

RINGS AND RINGLETS

The Voyager spacecraft confirmed that Saturn has a seventh ring. The probes found that the planet's seven rings are really thousands of separate ringlets. Each ringlet consists of billions of objects ranging in size from icebergs 33 feet wide to tiny specks of ice smaller than a pinhead. The three small moons found in Saturn's ring system were named Prometheus, Pandora, and Atlas. They help to keep all the parts of the rings in place by means of small gravitational forces. These small moons were nicknamed the "shepherd" moons.

moons in great detail and its cloud bands. The next visitor to Saturn will arrive in 2004, when the US orbiter *Cassini* will become the first spacecraft to orbit the planet. It will send the European *Huygens* probe to land on the

LANDING ON TITAN
The Cassini *spacecraft will carry the* Huygens *piggyback probe. The probe will parachute down onto the surface of Titan, Saturn's largest moon. Titan is one of the few moons in the Solar System to have an atmosphere.*

THE WORLD OF URANUS

 Voyager 2 arrived for a close encounter with Uranus on January 24, 1986, at a distance of 44,000 miles (71,000 km). Until then, very little was known about the planet or its newly discovered ring system. The visit by the Voyager spacecraft changed all that. It found 10 new moons, all of them inside the orbits of the five known satellites. Two new rings were discovered, and two of the new moons seemed to be acting as "shepherds", rather like those discovered in the rings of Saturn.

Little was revealed of the planet itself beneath its greenish-blue atmosphere of hydrogen and helium. Because *Voyager 2* was being targeted

RINGS AROUND URANUS
This combined image was taken by the remarkable Voyager 2 *spacecraft. It shows part of the moon, Miranda, as well as the planet's ring system and Uranus itself.*

at another destination, Neptune, the craft's close flight path across Uranus lasted only about 5 hours. Signals from *Voyager 2*, which was 1.79 billion miles (2.88 billion km) away, took 2 hours 25 minutes to reach the Earth.

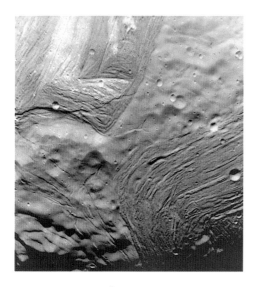

MIRANDA

Miranda is the smallest moon of Uranus. Its amazing surface is covered with a huge variety of features, including faults, grooves, terraces, and a steep cliff 10 miles (16 km) high.

FIVE MOONS

Voyager 2 made close-up images of the five known moons of Uranus: the cratered Oberon, bright Ariel, frosty Titania, dark Ombriel, and the amazing Miranda. Geologists have suggested that Miranda had fragmented at least a dozen times and re-formed in its present jumbled state, like a jigsaw puzzle put together in the wrong way. This theory may be linked to the fact that the rings of Uranus were found to consist of boulders rather than small particles. One of the ten new moons discovered, called Puck, was only 106 miles (170 km) across.

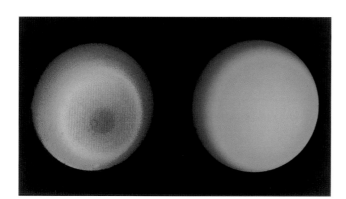

FALSE-COLOR VIEWS
Voyager 2's imaging system enabled it to take true and false-color views of Uranus. These highlighted the planet's atmospheric features and circulation patterns.

31

JOURNEY TO NEPTUNE

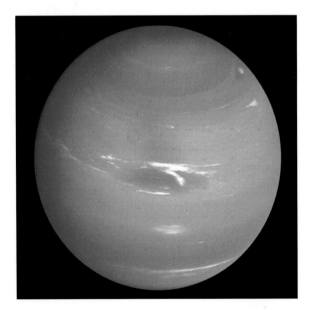

Voyager 2 sped past Neptune at 17 miles (27 km) per second on August 24, 1989. Radio signals from the spacecraft took 4 hours, 6 minutes to reach the Earth 2.78 billion miles (4.48 billion km) away. The signals arrived with the power equal to a fraction of one billionth of a watt. However, they contained an incredible mixture of data showing a blue planet with three main features: a Great Dark Spot, a wide band of clouds and white "scooter" clouds. The Great Dark Spot, which is the size of the Earth, circles around Neptune's equator every 18.3 hours, compared with the planet's own 19-hour rotation. The 2,680-mile (4,320-km) -wide band of clouds in the southern hemisphere has a Lesser Dark Spot. The "scooter" clouds travel at a speed of 400 miles (640 km) per hour.

Neptune was proving to be a more turbulent planet than its neighbor

"SCOOTER" CLOUDS
The Great Dark Spot rotates counter-clockwise as it travels around Neptune. It is accompanied by white "scooter" clouds which are between 30 miles (50 km) and 60 miles (100 km) above the main atmosphere.

THE LESSER DARK SPOT

This view of Neptune's southern hemisphere shows the Lesser Dark Spot. It seems to "change lanes" during every circuit in the wide cloud bands.

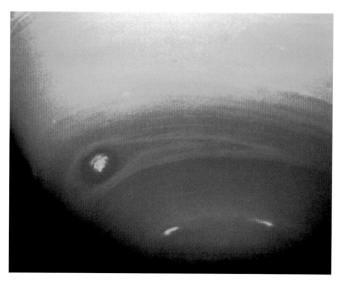

HALF AS BIG

The moon Triton, with a diameter of 1,860 miles (3,000 km), was only half the size that astronomers originally thought it was. Images of the moon revealed a surface of icy swamps of liquid nitrogen and methane, nitrogen frost clouds, mountains, craters and cliffs, quake faults, glaciers and geysers of liquid nitrogen. A surface temperature of −387 degrees F (−235 degrees C) makes Triton the coldest known place in the Solar System. Triton also displays glowing auroras caused by radiation trapped in Neptune's unique magnetic field. This radiation has also added a pinkish tinge to the moon's blue color.

Uranus. The "scooter" clouds orbit mainly around the equator. They are like the cirrus clouds found on the Earth, but are made of methane ice. *Voyager 2* also found a ring system and four new moons, as well as imaging the remarkable world of Triton.

TRITON

Neptune's largest moon, Triton, is an extraordinary icy world of nitrogen and methane. Geysers on the moon's surface throw out liquid nitrogen 25 miles (40 km) up into space.

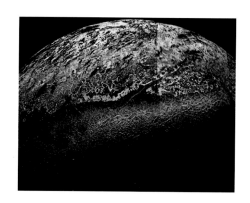

BEYOND OUR SYSTEM

Four spacecrafts — *Pioneer 10* and *11* and *Voyager 1* and *2* — are heading out of the Solar System and deeper into the Universe. At the end of 1998, *Pioneer 10* was about 6.55 billion miles (10.55 billion km) from the Earth traveling at a speed of 7 miles (12 km) per second. It is heading for the star Aldebaran 68 light-years away. It will take *Pioneer 10* 2 million years to reach the star. Contact with *Pioneer 11* has been lost.

It is is heading toward the constellation Aquila and may pass one of its stars in 4 million years' time.

Voyager 1 is the most distant artificial object in space. It is 6.7 billion miles (10.8 billion km) from the Earth and heading toward an encounter with a dwarf star in the constellation Camelopardus in 400,000 years' time. *Voyager 2* is 5.2 billion (8.4 billion km) from the Earth, heading for a flyby of Sirius, the brightest star in the Earth's skies, in about 358,000 years' time. Engineers hope to keep communicating with *Voyager 2* until at least 2010.

THE PIONEER AGE
Pioneer 10, which was launched in 1972 to visit Jupiter, is now heading toward the star Aldebaran in the constellation Taurus. The styles of the hair and clothing in this photograph show how much things have changed on Earth since the launch of Pioneer 10 *almost 30 years ago.*

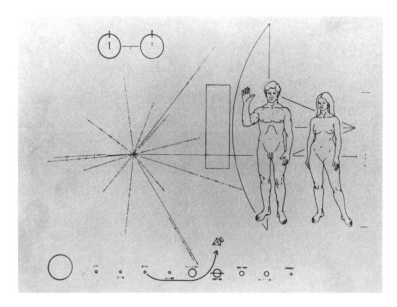

ON BOARD PIONEER

Pioneer 10 *carries a plaque that depicts a man and a woman and indicates the position of the planet Earth in space — just in case intelligent beings ever find the spacecraft.*

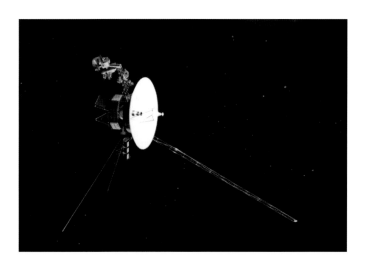

TO THE STARS

Voyager 1 *is the most distant artificial object heading out of the Solar System. Traveling at a speed of 10.5 miles (17 km) per second, it is now heading toward the stars.*

ROCKETS AND SATELLITES

Rocket technology made great advances following the end of World War II, based initially on Germany's V-2 guided missile. During the 1940s both the United States and the Soviet Union were launching research rockets, and by 1957 the Soviet Union was able to use a rocket to launch the first satellite into space. The first US satellite, *Explorer 1*, was launched the following year.

Today's generation of powerful rockets are used as launch vehicles

for a whole range of different probes and satellites. Satellites in orbit around the Earth make it possible for us to have instant telephone communications, receive TV pictures from the other side of the world, and exchange information via computer. Weather satellites monitor the world's weather, enabling forecasters to predict weather extremes such as hurricanes more accurately.

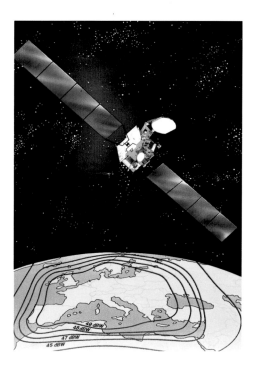

EARLY ROCKETS

Rockets that used a solid propellant such as gunpowder were launched by the Chinese as long ago as A.D.1200. However, the first liquid-propelled rocket was not launched until 1926, making the first major breakthrough in the development of space travel. The Soviet Union, the United States, and Germany began developing these rockets in the 1930s and the German *V-2* was put to deadly use in World War II. At the end of the war, many German rocket engineers went to the United States and the Soviet Union, helping these countries to make more powerful boosters. The *V-2* was modified to fly with the upper stage of a US Corporal rocket. The Viking, a highly successful US rocket became the basis for one of the first satellite launchers. The *V-2/Corporal*, nicknamed "Bumper", the *Viking* and *Aerobee* rockets, and many Soviet rockets were used to carry scientific instruments and animals into the lower reaches of space.

THE V-2 ROCKET
The V-2 rocket was developed by Germany during World War II. It fired over 3,000 missiles with deadly warheads. The rocket was later used by the USA to fly the first experiments into space.

UP AND DOWN

Another early space rocket was the Viking. Like the V-2, it flew an "up-and-down" flight, and not into orbit. It carried instruments that were later recovered after landing by parachute.

VIKING SERIES

The Viking high-altitude research rocket was launched 12 times, starting in 1949. One flight, *Viking 4*, was made from a ship. Its flight was typical of the missions flown by these booster rockets fueled by liquid oxygen and kerosene. *Viking 4* was used to measure atmospheric density, the speed of upper atmosphere winds, and cosmic-ray emissions, and to photograph the Earth from space. In 1954 *Viking 11* reached a record height of 156 miles (252 km) .

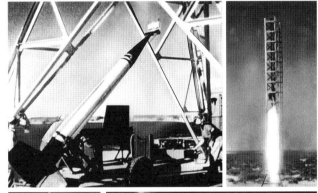

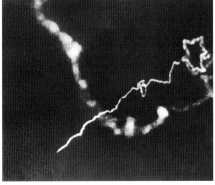

AEROBEE *ROCKET*

This Aerobee *rocket flew some of the first animals into space. The animals, such as mice, were recovered and examined to see how they had been affected by space travel.*

LAUNCHERS

By 1957, developing rocket technology had enabled the first Earth satellite, *Sputnik 1*, to be launched. Since then, all kinds of spacecraft have continued to provide a valuable service to the Earth. Science satellites help us to learn more about how the Earth is affected by solar winds and radiation. A fleet of weather satellites provides continuous monitoring of the whole Earth. Communications satellites span the globe providing television, radio, and telephone communications all over the world. The Internet could not exist without satellites.

Navigation satellites guide ships and aircrafts and even help to control the operation of commercial trucking. Environmental satellites survey the world's resources. Military satellites, including spy satellites, help to keep the peace. Space satellites help to run this age of high technology.

EUROPE'S ARIANE
The Ariane 5 *rocket will help Europe to continue to lead the commercial market for launching satellites into geostationary and other Earth orbits.*

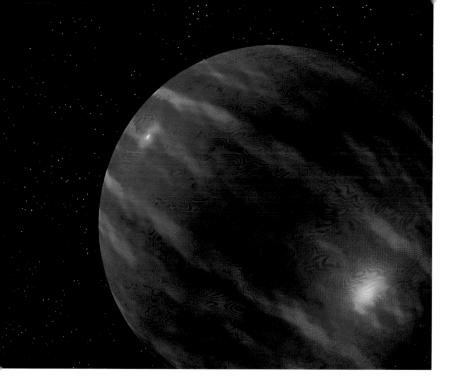

EARTH WATCH
Many different kinds of satellites are continually monitoring the Earth, providing data about its changing environment and resources.

THE SPACE BUSINESS

Space is big business, and governments are not the only organizations involved in it. Private companies build satellites and the launchers that put them into orbit. They also supply the infrastructure to allow services to be provided by the satellites. The cost of a typical communications satellite is $250 million. To launch it on a vehicle such as *Ariane 5* costs an extra $100 million. Further money is spent on insurance and the launch itself. So even before a satellite starts to work, it has cost about $500 million to put it in orbit.

MONITORING HURRICANES
Weather satellites provide a vital service by detecting the birth and development of hurricanes. These satellites plot the path of a hurricane so that early warnings can be given to people living in the affected areas.

41

SATELLITE TECHNOLOGY

Communications satellite technology has developed at a rapid rate. Just 30 years ago the rather basic Telstar satellite was transmitting TV signals to a ground station for onward transmission by land line to people's homes. Today, satellites can beam TV pictures directly into millions of homes — and from not just one channel but hundreds of different ones at the same time. Some important scientific advances have made this possible. First, we can now produce miniature components, such as traveling wave tube amplifiers. Also the satellites, with their perfectly

fashioned antennas, have extremely high transmitting power — they are supplied with large amounts of electricity by advanced solar panels. Lastly, the high power transmissions

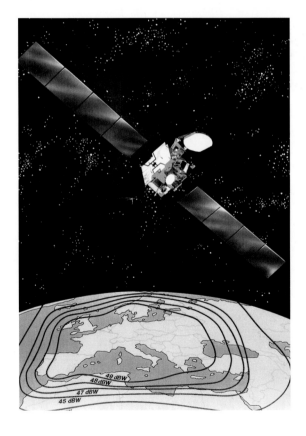

SIGNALS FROM SPACE
The antennas of communications satellites are "aimed" at specific user areas, called footprints. In these areas, highly amplified high-power signals are received by "dishes" that are as small as dinner plates.

mean that satellite receiving dishes can be smaller. Satellites provide numerous communications services other than television. Some are able to handle 30,000 simultaneous phone, data, and fax calls.

SATELLITE SYSTEMS

The Iridium satellite system uses 66 operational satellites in a low orbit above the Earth. The satellites are positioned in such a way that a mobile phone user is within "line of sight" of at least one satellite at any time.

SATELLITE POWER

The 155-pound (77-kg) Telstar satellite, with solar cells providing 15 watts of electricity, used to transmit to a single receiving dish with a diameter of 82 feet (25 m). Today, a typical communications satellite weighs 7,700 pounds (3,500 kg) and has 30 amplifiers providing high power transmission in many wavebands. Using 6,000 watts of power from solar cells, it transmits to thousands of receiving dishes as small as 3 feet (90 cm) in diameter.

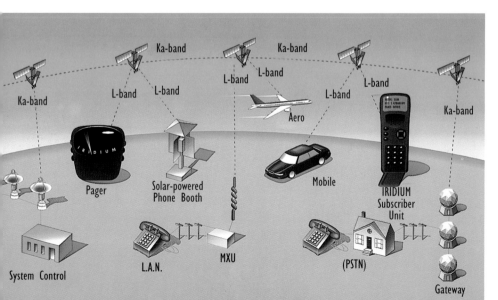

Ka-band · Ka-band · Ka-band
L-band · L-band
Ka-band · L-band · L-band · L-band
Aero · L-band · Ka-band
Pager · Solar-powered Phone Booth · Mobile · IRIDIUM Subscriber Unit
System Control · L.A.N. · MXU · (PSTN) · Gateway

COMMUNICATING ON THE MOVE

Modern communications technology allows us to keep in touch with each other from almost anywhere in the world. The network of satellites in space provides instant communications whether by telephone, mobile phone, fax, pager, computer, or e-mail.

43

NAVIGATION SATELLITES

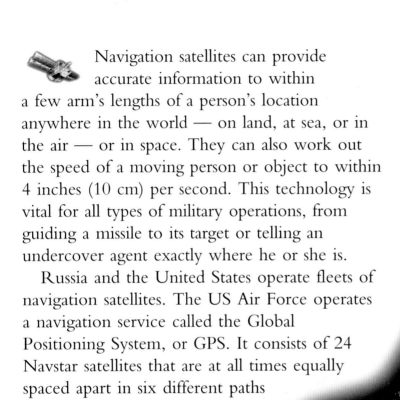

Navigation satellites can provide accurate information to within a few arm's lengths of a person's location anywhere in the world — on land, at sea, or in the air — or in space. They can also work out the speed of a moving person or object to within 4 inches (10 cm) per second. This technology is vital for all types of military operations, from guiding a missile to its target or telling an undercover agent exactly where he or she is.

Russia and the United States operate fleets of navigation satellites. The US Air Force operates a navigation service called the Global Positioning System, or GPS. It consists of 24 Navstar satellites that are at all times equally spaced apart in six different paths around the Earth.

NAVSTAR SATELLITE LAUNCH
An American Delta II *booster is launched from Cape Canaveral. It is carrying a Navstar communications satellite into its circular 13,133-mile (21,182-km) orbit.*

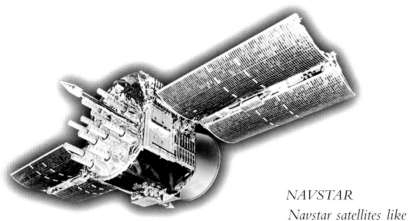

NAVSTAR

Navstar satellites like this one provide vital positioning information for all kinds of uses, from guiding a military fighter through the skies to helping lost sailors find their way at sea.

HOW GPS WORKS

Each GPS satellite continually transmits its position and the exact time of its transmission. A receiver on an aircraft or ship or carried by a hiker, for example, receives signals from four satellites at the same time. The receiver processes the data and displays the user's position and speed and the exact time. GPS has become a vital part of worldwide search and rescue. A search beacon on a liferaft in the middle of the ocean can be located and positioned accurately by GPS satellites.

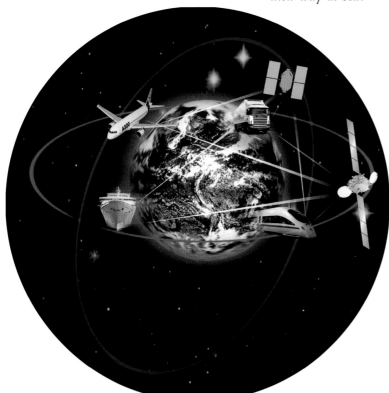

TRAFFIC CONTROL

Navigation technology that was originally developed for the military has now been transferred into the civilian sector. Soon even airlines will rely on satellites for air traffic control.

45

INTRODUCTION TO

SPACE PROGRAMS

After the success of the first satellites in space, both the United States and Soviet Union embarked on their own space programs. The main part of each program consisted of a series of manned space flights. The Soviet Union's powerful rockets allowed them to launch large well-equipped spacecrafts able to sustain cosmonauts in space for several days. Meanwhile, the United States led the way with satellite technology

and also in the race to the Moon, which they eventually won.

The first flight of the Apollo Moon program took place in October 1968. In December 1968, the three astronauts on board *Apollo 8* orbited the Moon 10 times. By July of the following year, the first person had set foot on the surface of the Moon. American astronauts made five further landings on the Moon between 1969 and 1972.

RACE TO THE MOON

 In 1961 President John F. Kennedy decided to respond to the Soviet "threat" of dominance in space. He announced to the US Congress on May 25, that he wanted his country to land men on the Moon before 1970. The space project would cost more than $25 billion and would require a series of manned space flights to prove the technology, and Moon scouts to check out the new territory. What became known as Project Apollo was one of the most extraordinary undertakings of the twentieth century. It was undertaken on the assumption that the Soviet Union was also planning to send men to the Moon, so the "space race" became known as the "Moon race."

Space flight dominated the 1960s, hardly ever leaving the front pages of newspapers as important steps in the Apollo project were taken year by year. These events led up to the momentous first manned landing on the Moon in July 1969.

FIRST AMERICAN IN SPACE
Twenty-three days after Soviet cosmonaut Yuri Gagarin became the first person in space, Alan Shepard became the first American in space in the Mercury capsule Freedom 7.

SHEPARD'S SPLASHDOWN
US astronaut Alan Shepard is hauled aboard a helicopter
after completing his 15 minute up-and-down space flight
with a planned splashdown in the Atlantic Ocean.

A NATION ON THE MOON

President Kennedy said:
"I believe that this nation should commit itself to achieving the goal, before this decade is out, of landing a man on the Moon and returning him safely to Earth. No single space project in this period will be more exciting, or more expensive to mankind, or more important for the long-range exploration of space; and none will be so difficult or expensive to accomplish. … It will not be one man going to the Moon … it will be an entire nation.

MAN ON THE MOON
President Kennedy's goal was to place an American on the Moon by 1969. When he announced the Moon project, the USA had just 15 minutes of manned space flight experience.

FIRST APOLLO FLIGHTS

 After the three-man crew of *Apollo 7* successfully tested the command and service modules in Earth orbit, a decision was made to send *Apollo 8* to the Moon. The Unite States feared that the Soviet Union was about to send two cosmonauts around the Moon on a fly-by mission. So the planned *Apollo 8* lunar module test flight in Earth orbit was canceled. Instead, *Apollo 8* was sent to make 10 orbits of the Moon. The mission was one of the biggest milestones in space history and one of the major events of the twentieth century.

The three astronauts in *Apollo 8* were launched on December 21, 1968. While orbiting the Moon over Christmas they sent back messages

LAUNCH OF APOLLO 7
A smaller Saturn 1B *rocket boosts* Apollo 7 *into orbit on the first manned flight of the Apollo space program. The three-man crew made a successful 11-day flight, proving the command and service module systems.*

of goodwill and read from the Bible. *Apollo 8* came to within 66 miles (110 km) of the Moon's surface. The memorable flight ended with a safe splashdown in the Pacific Ocean — and the astronauts brought back the first photo of the rising Earth as seen from the Moon.

MOON CRATER
The first close look at the Moon was made during the Apollo 8 *mission. This is the crater Langrenus taken by* Apollo 8*'s photographer, Bill Anders, while orbiting the Moon.*

CREW OF APOLLO 8
The first men to fly to the Moon were Frank Borman, James Lovell, and Bill Anders. They made 10 orbits of the Moon in their Apollo 8 *spacecraft during Christmas 1968.*

MAN ON THE MOON

Eight years after President Kennedy's pledge to land an American on the Moon, *Apollo 11* was ready to do just that. Millions of people all over the world followed one of the most historic events in the history of the human race — the first steps on another body in space. The actual landing was a nail-biting affair as several computer alarms threatened to end it. Flight commander Neil Armstrong had to take manual control to stop the lunar module landing in a rocky crater. He landed with just seconds of fuel left.

FIRST STEPS ON THE MOON
Buzz Aldrin comes down the ladder to set foot on the lunar dust at Tranquillity Base. This photo was taken by his fellow astronaut Neil Armstrong.

Thanks to satellite technology, millions were able to follow events live on TV. The high point was watching the first walk on the Moon, as Armstrong's ghostly looking figure stepped off the footpad of the lunar module *Eagle*. He was followed by Buzz Aldrin, and both set to work deploying two science instruments and collecting samples of rock to bring back to Earth. The third *Apollo 11* astronaut, Mike Collins, stayed on board the command module.

APOLLO 11*'S CREW*
Neil Armstrong (left), Michael Collins (center) and Buzz Aldrin (right) pose for a formal crew portrait a few weeks before the launch of their epic Apollo 11 *mission to the Moon.*

MOON MISQUOTES
No one knew what Neil Armstrong was going to say when he placed his right boot onto the lunar surface. He only decided finally after he had landed safely. He said that he didn't see the point in worrying about what to say when he didn't know whether he would land successfully — he believed that they had a 50-50 chance of success. Unfortunately, Armstrong's remark became one of the most misquoted in history. He meant to say, "That's one small step for a man, one giant leap for mankind." He actually said, "That's one small step for man, one giant leap for mankind."

53

SHUTTLES AND STATIONS

When the first Space Shuttle took off in 1981, it marked a major milestone in the history of space exploration. With its ability to land back on Earth like an airplane, the Shuttle is the first manned spacecraft that can be reused. It has made an important contribution to satellite technology. Shuttle astronauts not only deploy communications and other satellites in space, but they even retrieve and repair damaged ones while remaining in space. The Hubble Space

Telescope, which has sent back so many spectacular images of space, was deployed by the Shuttle.

The Space Shuttle has also ferried astronauts to the *Mir* space station, launched by the Soviet Union in 1986. Extra modules have been added to extend the station. *Mir* has received astronauts and scientists from many different countries. The first parts of a new international space station were assembled in space in 1998.

THE SPACE SHUTTLE

The Space Shuttle consists of three main parts: the orbiter spaceplane, two solid rocket boosters, and an external propellant tank. The shuttle is launched using three main engines attached to the orbiter. The engines are fed with propellants from the external tank (ET) and by two solid propellant strap-on solid rocket boosters (SRB). The SRBs use up their fuel after 2 minutes and are ejected. They are recovered for reuse in later flights. The orbiter and its ET continue flying for 6 more minutes until the initial orbit is reached. The ET is then jettisoned. The orbiter's orbital maneuvering system (OMS) engines and reaction control system (RCS) thrusters are used to change the orbit and perform maneuvers.

At the end of the flight, the OMS engines are fired and the orbiter plunges into the Earth's atmosphere at 25 times the speed of sound. The friction causes its 34,000 heat shield tiles to heat up to 2,880 degrees Fahrenheit (1,600 degrees Celsius). The orbiter then lands like a glider.

orbiter

solid rocket booster

external tank

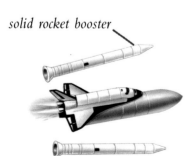

SHUTTLE LAUNCH
Two minutes after the Shuttle takes off, the solid rocket boosters are ejected and fall back to Earth by parachute. Six minutes later, the external tank is jettisoned and is destroyed as it reenters the Earth's atmosphere.

ASSEMBLING THE SHUTTLE
The Space Shuttle is assembled vertically inside the Vehicle Assembly Building at the Kennedy Space Center. It is rolled out to the launch pad on a mobile launch platform.

"FLYING BRICK"

The orbiter makes a carefully controlled approach to its landing site. It descends at an angle seven times steeper than that of a normal airliner, with a nose-down angle of 28 degrees. The vehicle finally lands at a speed of more than 200 miles per hour (300 km/h).

The Shuttle has been nicknamed by astronauts as the "flying brick". The commander and pilot of Shuttle missions make hundreds of practice landings using a specially adapted training aircraft.

LANDING OPERATIONS
Immediately after landing, the orbiter is surrounded by a crowd of vehicles and engineers. They prepare it for transfer to the Shuttle Processing Facility where the orbiter is made ready for its next flight.

SKYLAB

Launched in 1973, *Skylab* was America's first and so far only space station — until the launch of the first American section of the International Space Station 25 years later. Much of *Skylab* was made of equipment developed for the Apollo program. Its main orbital workshop comprised a fully equipped empty upper stage of a *Saturn V* rocket. The Apollo telescope mount was based on a leftover lunar module. *Skylab* was launched using a *Saturn V* rocket, and crews were sent to the space station aboard Apollo command service modules that docked with the space station.

Three crews were launched to *Skylab*, consisting of several astronauts who would have flown later Apollo missions that had been canceled. Each crew included one scientist astronaut. The first crew had to repair the space station after it was damaged during launch. The final crew stayed in the space station for 84 days.

SKYLAB *DAMAGE*
Skylab *was damaged during launch and lost one of its solar panels. Another panel was successfully deployed during a brave space walk, saving the whole* Skylab *program.*

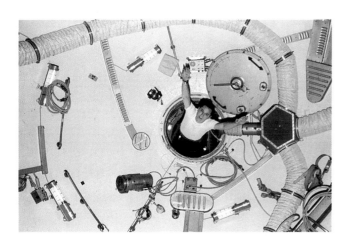

FLOATING AROUND
Scientist astronaut Edward Gibson floats into the orbital workshop during the third and last Skylab mission in 1973 and 1974. It lasted 84 days, which was an American record.

SCIENTIFIC STUDY
Skylab was a fully equipped science base, with one section devoted to astronomy and the study of the Sun. Here, scientist Gibson mans the operating console for the telescope.

THE MIR SPACE STATION

 The *Mir* space station is Russia's extraordinary success story. It was still operating in 1999 13 years after the launch of its first module. The space station consists of the *Mir* core module and a small *Kvant 1* module attached to its rear. Soyuz manned spacecraft and Progress unmanned tankers can dock at a port on the *Kvant 1* module. Attached to the front of the core module is a docking module with five ports. One is used for Soyuz ferries and the other four are for modules that were launched later. The whole space station, with six modules, a Progress tanker and a Soyuz spacecraft, weighs about 130 tons.

WORKING TOGETHER
Russian cosmonaut Yuri Gidzenko and German astronaut Thomas Reiter at work on board the Mir *space station in 1996. The two men also went on space walks together.*

FOREIGN ASTRONAUTS

Thomas Reiter, a German astronaut representing the European Space Agency, flew a 179-day mission on *Mir*. Six American astronauts, including Shannon Lucid and Michael Foale, have also stayed on *Mir* for more than 100 days. France has also flown commercial missions on the space station. One of the French astronauts was Jean Loup Chretien who also flew on *Salyut 7* — and revisited *Mir* in a Space Shuttle! Shorter missions have been flown by other countries, including Afghanistan and Syria.

Mir has hosted almost 30 main crews, including one cosmonaut who stayed on board for a record 437 days. In addition, many visiting crews have included astronauts from other countries, including the United States, the UK and Germany. Foreign countries have paid Russia for the scientific experiment time on board and for the space flight experience.

INDEX

ACKNOWLEDGMENTS

The publishers wish to thank the following artists who have
contributed to this book.

Julian Baker, Kuo Kang Chen, Rob Jakeway, Darrell Warner
(Beehive Illustrations) Guy Smith, Janos Marffy,
Peter Sarson.

Photographs supplied by Genesis Photo Library and
Miles Kelly Archive.

FANTASTIC FACTS ABOUT

STARS & PLANETS

Author
Tim Furniss

Editor
Steve Parker

Design
Pentacor

Image Coordination
Ian Paulyn

Production Assistant
Rachel Jones

Index
Jane Parker

Editorial Director
Paula Borton

Design Director
Clare Sleven

Publishing Director
Jim Miles

This is a Parragon Publishing Book

This edition is published in 2001

Parragon Publishing, Queen Street House, 4 Queen Street, Bath BA1 1HE, UK

Copyright Parragon © 2000

Parragon has previously printed this material in 1999 as part of the Factfinder series

2 4 6 8 10 9 7 5 3 1

Produced by Miles Kelly Publishing Ltd
Bardfield Centre, Great Bardfield, Essex CM7 4SL

ISBN 0-75254-879-4

Printed in China

FANTASTIC FACTS ABOUT

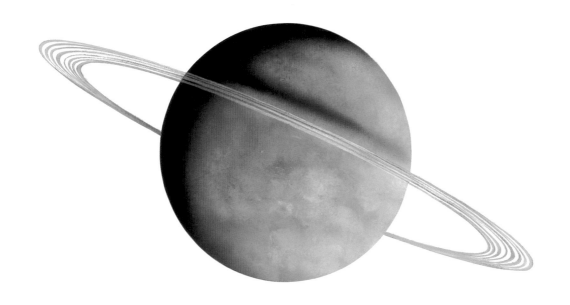

STARS & PLANETS

p

CONTENTS

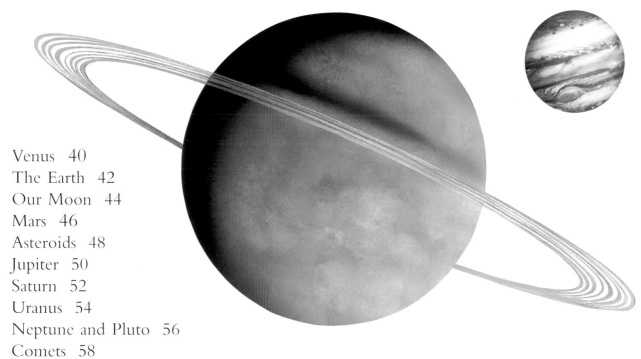

INTRODUCTION

There are few subjects more interesting than the night sky, with its constellations of stars and planets. Earth is the only planet where life is known to exist, and the Sun is merely a medium-sized star among millions in the Milky Way galaxy. Now, thanks to modern technology, we are just beginning to understand some of the mysteries of the ever-expanding Universe.

STARS AND PLANETS is a handy reference guide in the *Fascinating Facts* series. Each book has been specially compiled with a collection of stunning illustrations and photographs which bring the subject to life. Hundreds of facts and figures are presented in a variety of interesting ways and fact-panels which provide information at-a-glance. This unique combination is fun and easy to use and makes learning a pleasure.

OUR EARTH

Ever since the first humans peered in wonder at the stars in the night sky, we have longed to know more about the Universe. Today, we have the technology to explore deeper into the Universe than ever imagined. The Earth is just one very tiny part of the vast Universe — a small rocky planet traveling around a medium-sized star, the Sun, in one of billions of galaxies. Nobody really knows where the Universe begins or ends. Even though the most powerful radio telescope has detected a quasar 13.2 billion light-years away, we have so far explored only a very small part of the Universe.

THE EARTH AND ITS MOON
This is a view of the Earth as seen from another world in space — from our neighbor, the Moon. This classic photograph of the space age was taken by the crew of Apollo 8 *in December 1968.*

For around 400 years, most of our knowledge about the night sky and "what is out there" came from light telescopes. There are two main kinds: refracting telescopes which use only lenses (far left), and reflecting telescopes which use mirrors and lenses (near left). From the 1930s, radio telescopes were able to detect other rays and waves from space.

FARTHER THAN EVER

Scientists believe that the Universe is expanding all the time. Groups of galaxies are rushing away from our Milky Way Galaxy, and also from each other. As a result, the distances between galaxies are increasing, and the Universe is getting bigger and bigger. The stars within these galaxies are slowly changing too, and new ones are constantly forming. The huge columns of cool interstellar gas and dust known as nebulae are the birthplaces of new stars. The Eagle Nebula, also known as M16, is in the constellation Serpens in the northern sky. Its tallest pillar is one light-year long, and our whole Solar System could be swallowed up inside one of the "fingertips" at the top of the column.

PLANETS AND MOONS
A montage of images taken by NASA's Voyager 1 *and* 2 *spacecraft shows the beautiful ringed planet Saturn and a few of its many moons.*

DISTANT NEBULA
This awe-inspiring image from the
Hubble Space Telescope shows the
Eagle Nebula, which is 7,000 light-
years away from the Earth.

THE UNIVERSE

The Universe is everything that exists.
It stretches farther almost than the human
mind can imagine — we already know
that the Universe reaches at over 13
billion light-years in every direction.
The Universe is filled with matter
in many different shapes, sizes, and
forms. It contains dust and gases;
planets such as the Earth and
Jupiter; the Sun and billions of
other stars; our Milky Way Galaxy
and countless galaxies.

Our tiny planet Earth has a unique place in the Universe because it is the only place where we know that life definitely exists. There is still so much for us to discover about the vast Universe — about how it began and where it might end. One day we might even discover life in other parts of our Universe, or even the existence of other universes.

HOME IN THE COSMOS

We can begin to understand the size of the Universe, and our place in it, by writing an address such as this: Jane Smith, Human Being, 5 Robins Avenue, Libertyville, North Dakota, United States, North America, The Earth, The Solar System, The Milky Way, Galaxy Group C7, The Universe. The Earth is one of nine planets that move round the Sun, forming what we call the Solar System. The Sun is just one of more than 100 billion stars in a galaxy that we call the Milky Way. The Milky Way is just one of millions of other galaxies in the vast Universe.

The Earth is a unique part of the Universe since it is the only place where we know that life definitely exists. This life is not just small microbes but a life of incredible variety. About 5 billion human beings live on Earth, yet we are just one kind of being among more than 1 million different species.

14

THE BEGINNING OF TIME

The powerful Hubble Space Telescope is able to look back into the "beginning of time." This image reveals a small number of the countless multicolored galaxies of all shapes and sizes that are found in the Universe.

HORSEHEAD NEBULA

The Horsehead Nebula is a cloud of cool dust. Here it is seen rising up against a backdrop of hot gas. The gas is glowing with energy from nearby stars.

THE VAST UNIVERSE

The image (above left) from the Hubble Space Telescope shows a part of our night sky. It covers an area that is just 1/30th the size of the Moon as we see it in the sky. Some of the galaxies are so far away that they are up to four billion times fainter than the limits of human vision. Although this image covers a very small area of the sky, it shows a typical arrangement of galaxies in space. In fact, from a statistical point of view the Universe looks the same in every direction.

SUN AND SOLAR SYSTEM

The Sun is a very ordinary star among billions of other stars in the Milky Way Galaxy. It has a planetary system, called the Solar System, which is made up of planets and other "left–over" material that did not form into planets. The nine known planets start with Mercury, which is at an average distance of 35.9 million miles (57.9 million km) from the Sun. Then comes Venus, the Earth, Mars, Jupiter, Saturn, Uranus, Neptune, and Pluto. Between the orbits of Mars and Jupiter lies an area of one kind of leftover material, the asteroids. These are lumps of

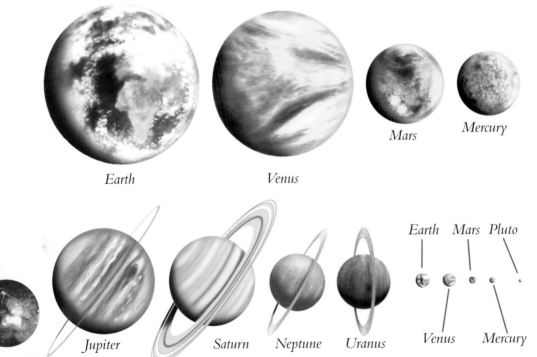

Earth

Venus

Mars

Mercury

Jupiter

Saturn

Neptune

Uranus

Earth   Mars   Pluto

Venus   Mercury

THE PLANETS OF THE SOLAR SYSTEM
This montage shows all the planets of the Solar System, compared in size. Mercury, the planet nearest to the Sun, is on the left, and Earth is third from the left. Jupiter is the largest planet. Pluto, the ninth and last planet, is almost too small to see.

rock, some of which are many miles long. Beyond Pluto is another kind of leftover material, the comets. These are bodies of rock, ice, and dust. When some comets pass close to the Sun they heat up and give off material, forming a tail. Comets also give off small rocky particles that form many of the meteors, or "shooting stars," that we see.

THE PLANETS AT A GLANCE

Planet	Average distance from Sun	Diameter
Mercury	35.9 million miles	3,026 miles
Venus	67 million miles	7,500 miles
Earth	92.8 million miles	7,909 miles
Mars	141.3 million miles	4,146 miles
Jupiter	482.5 million miles	88,536 miles
Saturn	884.7 million miles	73,966 miles
Uranus	1.78 billion miles	32,116 miles
Neptune	2.79 billion miles	30,690 miles
Pluto	3.66 billion miles	1,550 miles

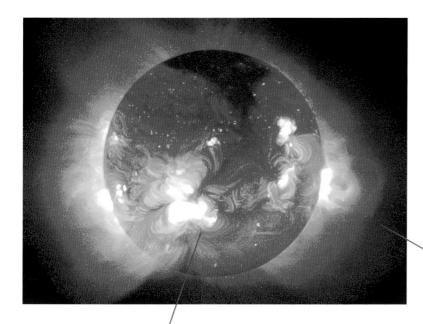

SUPER-HOT SUN
If we had X-ray eyes, this is how the Sun would look to us. This image shows the Sun's turbulent atmosphere. In the outer layer, or corona, temperatures reach as high as 2.6 million degrees Fahrenheit (2 million degrees Celsius).

The corona is the outer layer of the Sun's atmosphere

The photosphere, or surface, of the Sun

17

THE SPEED OF LIGHT

As we know, our Earth is a very small but rather important part of the vast Universe. The Universe is so huge that we cannot measure it in miles or kilometers, or even millions of them. Imagine writing down in miles or kilometers the distance of the Andromeda Galaxy from Earth. It would take millions of numbers — far too many to fit on a page of this book. So astronomers measure the size of the Universe or the distance of stars by using the speed at which light from these objects travels. Light travels in empty space at a speed of 185,871 miles (299,792 km) per second. (It travels a little slower when passing through water, glass or other denser media.) The distance that light travels in one year — 5.88 trillion miles (9.46 trillion km) — is called a light-year. Light from the Sun, which is about 93 million miles (150 million km) from Earth, takes 8 minutes to reach us. The nearest star, Proxima Centauri, is 4.225 light-years from Earth.

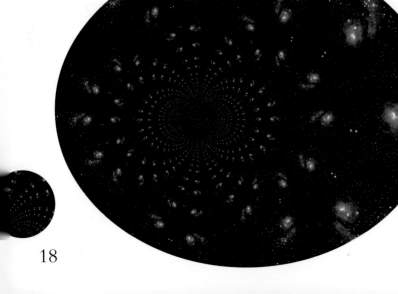

LIGHT ON THE MOVE
Light from the most distant galaxy so far detected in the Universe took 13.1 trillion years to reach the Earth. Light from the Sun takes just 8 minutes!

A LIGHT-YEAR

A light-year is a measure of distance, not time. It is written as 5,831,571,200,000,000,000 miles (9,500,000,000,000 km). The Moon is 238,328 miles (384,400 km) from the Earth. It took astronauts about 3 days to travel to the Moon. How long would it have taken those astronauts to travel to the brightest star Sirius? If Sirius is 8.6 light-years away, that's the same as 503,371,500,000,000,000,000 miles (811,899,530,000,000,000,000 km) After 63,363,030,000,000,000 days, or 173,597,340,000,000 years, they would reach Sirius!

THE MILKY WAY

These are some of the stars in our Milky Way Galaxy. The brightest star in our night sky is also one of the nearest. It is called Sirius, in the constellation Canis Major, and is 8.6 light-years away from Earth.

THE ANDROMEDA GALAXY

The nearest galaxy to our Milky Way Galaxy is the spectacular Andromeda Galaxy. It can just be seen with the naked eye as a small fuzzy patch of light in the northern skies, near the constellation Pegasus.

19

THE MILKY WAY

THE MILKY WAY GALAXY
No one knows exactly what the Milky Way Galaxy looks like from the outside. It is a spiral-shaped galaxy, with arms that resemble the shape of a spinning firework.

We can see about 5,000 individual stars in the night sky. On a really clear night, it is also possible to see one or two galaxies. The most visible part of our own Milky Way Galaxy is the part of the sky that looks like a misty cloud. It is really a band of millions of stars. This part of our Galaxy that we can actually see is also called the Milky Way. When we look at it, we are looking towards the center of our Galaxy where there are the most stars. We cannot actually see the center because we are situated a long way from the center in the Orion arm, an outer arm of the Galaxy. When we look at the region where the famous Orion constellation is situated, there seem to be fewer stars. This is because we are looking toward the edge of the Galaxy.

Halley's Comet

HALLEY'S COMET

This photo of the Milky Way also shows Halley's Comet passing across the sky. A comet orbits the Sun, and so it is much closer to Earth than the distant stars.

OUR GALAXY

If we could look at it from the side, the Milky Way Galaxy would be a rather thin disk with a dense, bulging center surrounded by a halo. This halo is a mass of older stars surrounding the central mass, which contains the most stars. The thinner edges of the disk are the outer arms of the Galaxy. The Milky Way Galaxy is about 2,000 light-years thick but 100,000 light-years across. It contains an estimated 100,000 million stars. Our Sun, which is one of those stars, is about 30,000 light-years from the center. It orbits the center of the Galaxy at a speed of 170 miles (274 km) per second.

BIRTH OF THE STARS

In addition to the millions of stars in the Milky Way Galaxy, there are also many nebulae, which are regions where stars are being born. This is a nebula in the constellation Cygnus.

GALAXIES AND NEBULAE

 When we look into the night sky, we can observe other objects in addition to stars. Some, like nebulae, are inside the Milky Way, while others are distant galaxies much farther away. The most famous nebula is part of the constellation Orion (the Hunter). Hanging from the hunter's "belt" of three stars is a "sword" of stars. In the middle of the sword is the Orion Nebula, a region of hot gas and dust where new stars are born. The nebula is 1,500 light-years away and 15 light-years across.

The most famous galaxy is the Andromeda Galaxy, which is close to the constellation Pegasus. It is the most distant object visible to the naked eye and looks like a small fuzzy

Central band of dust and cloud

SOMBRERO GALAXY
This is a spectacular, almost perfectly formed galaxy called the Sombrero Galaxy. It is also called a nebula because it has a prominent central band of dust and cloud.

patch. The Andromeda Galaxy is a huge spiral galaxy, 2.2 billion light-years away. It is thought to contain at least 300 billion stars.

DYING STARS

Some nebulae are the remnants of dying stars. The mysterious "searchlight" beams emerging from a hidden star in the Egg Nebula (left) are being crisscrossed by many bright arcs. The nebula is a huge cloud of dust and gas ejected by a dying star. The star, which is hidden by a dense cocoon of dust, is expanding at a speed of 12 miles (20 km) per second. Eventually the dying star will blow off its outer layers to form a planetary nebula.

The Egg Nebula is a swirling cloud of gas and dust

EGG NEBULA

This strange-looking nebula, called the Egg Nebula, is 3,000 light-years away from Earth. This photo was taken by the Hubble Space Telescope, which has helped to revolutionize astronomy.

THE VAST UNIVERSE

Scientists estimate that there are billions of galaxies in the Universe, but we cannot be sure because no one knows where the Universe ends — if it does! People who believe that the Universe was created by a god or gods can accept that it is beyond our human understanding. There are also many people who believe that the Universe was not created but just "happened," perhaps in a "big bang"; its glory was simply an accident. Whatever people think, the human race will perhaps never fully understand the nature of the Universe. However, this lack of understanding will not stop us from

SPACE AND TIME

Space is not straight, continuous, or constant. Neither is time. In the relationship between space and time, space curves around massive objects, such as stars, while time speeds up or slows down. The Universe is filled with mysterious objects such as black holes, and perhaps even "short-cuts," or wormholes, to other dimensions or even other universes.

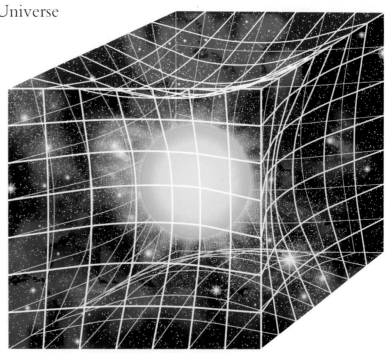

trying to find out more about the Universe, through observation and exploration. Yet each new and exciting discovery seems to create even more questions to be answered!

THE VAST UNIVERSE
We may only be able to see a very small section of a much larger Universe. The size of the Universe is so great that human beings can only begin to perceive it.

EVERYTHING THAT EXISTS
The Universe contains everything that exists. It contains all of space, time and matter. There could be millions of other galaxies like our Milky Way in the Universe. The most distant galaxy that we have detected so far is over 13 million light-years away.

BIGGER AND FARTHER

In 1990, astronomers discovered a galaxy called Abell 2029 in the constellation Virgo. The Abell 2029 Galaxy is 1,070 million light-years away and has an incredible diameter of 5.6 million light-years, which is 80 times bigger than the Milky Way. The most remote object yet discovered in the Universe is over 13 million light-years away and is a quasar inside a galaxy. Quasars are mysterious space objects which are thought to be associated with equally mysterious black holes.

SIGNPOSTS IN THE SKY

Long ago, people divided up the night sky into distinct areas called constellations. The word "constellation" also refers to a pattern of stars that appears in a particular area of the sky. Many of these star patterns are named after animals or figures from mythology.

Astronomers have named a total of 88 different constellations. The most famous one in the night sky of the northern hemisphere is probably Ursa Major, or the Great Bear. It contains a well-known group of stars called the Big Dipper. Even people who are not interested in astronomy can usually locate the Big Dipper easily. It is sometimes described as being like a saucepan with a bent handle. It has four main stars which form an outline rather like that of a saucepan. The bent handle consists of another three main stars.

Polaris, or Pole Star

The Big Dipper

THE BIG DIPPER

The Big Dipper makes a wonderful signpost in the sky. The two stars on the right-hand side of the saucepan point up to a star called Polaris. This is the Pole Star, the nearest star to the place in the northern skies to which the Earth's axis points. Because the Earth rotates on its own axis, the Pole Star looks as if it remains in the same place in the sky as the other stars move around it.

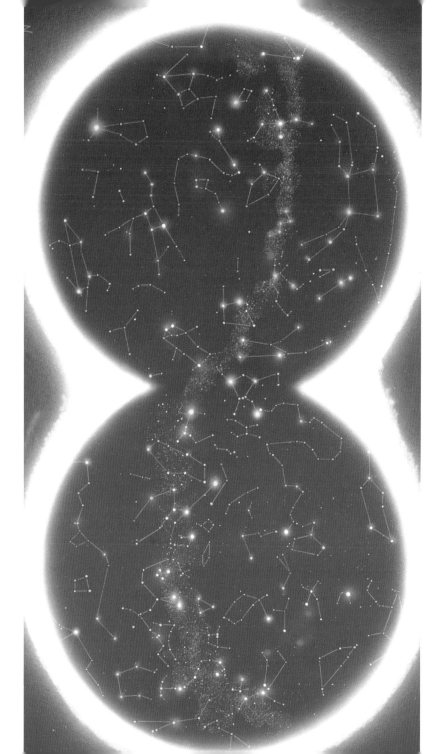

ORION AND PEGASUS

The magnificent constellation Orion dominates the winter sky in the northern hemisphere. Not only can it be used as a signpost, but it is also one of the constellations that really seems to look like the character it depicts—the Hunter. We can clearly make out his belt and sword, and to the right his bent bow and arrow pointing at the horns of an angry bull—Taurus. The Orion Nebula is visible within the third star of the Hunter's sword. The famous Andromeda Galaxy can be located using the almost perfect "square" set of stars in the constellation Pegasus.

THE NIGHT SKIES

This map shows the stars and constellations of the northern (top) and southern (bottom) hemispheres. The sky in the northern hemisphere is shown as it appears from the North Pole. Polaris, the Pole Star, is directly overhead. There is no equivalent of the Pole Star in the southern hemisphere.

27

BRIGHTEST STARS

 The measure of a star's brightness is called its magnitude. The smaller the magnitude, the brighter the star is. The first person to work out a level of brightness was probably a Greek astronomer called Hipparchus. He divided the stars as he could see them into six groups. The stars in the brightest group were first magnitude, and the faintest stars were sixth magnitude. Later, other astronomers worked out that Hipparchus's brightest stars were about 100 times brighter than sixth-magnitude stars. The stars that were 100 times brighter than sixth magnitude were given a minus number, and the fainter ones were given a plus number. One of the brightest stars, Arcturus, the main star of the constellation Boötes, has a magnitude of –0.06.

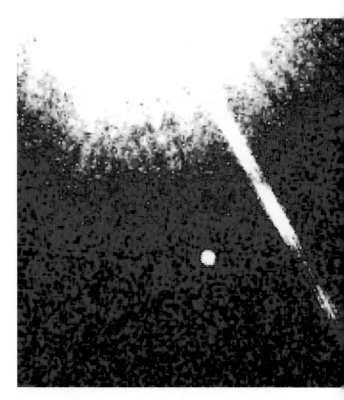

STAR BRIGHT
This dramatic picture shows a high-resolution image of a star. Out of the 14 brightest stars in the night sky, 11 of them are visible in the northern hemisphere.

WITH THE NAKED EYE

We can see about 5,000 stars in the night sky with the naked eye. Fainter stars can be seen only with binoculars or telescopes.

Betelgeuse

THE 14 BRIGHTEST STARS

Star	Constellation	Magnitude
Sirius	Canis Major	−1.45
Canopus	Carina	−0.73
Alpha Centauri	Centaurus	−0.1
Arcturus	Boötes	−0.06
Vega	Lyra	−0.04
Capella	Auriga	−0.08
Rigel	Orion	−0.11
Procyon	Canis Minor	+0.35
Achernar	Eridanus	+0.48
Beta Centauri	Centaurus	+0.6
Altair	Aquila	+0.77
Betelgeuse	Orion	+0.8
Aldebaran	Taurus	+0.85
Acrux	Crux	+0.09

BETELGEUSE

Betelgeuse, in the constellation Orion, is an old and dying red giant star. This picture was taken by the Hubble Space Telescope. Betelgeuse is about 310 light-years away from Earth. It has a diameter of about 300 million miles (500 million km) and could swallow up the Solar System almost as far as the planet Jupiter.

MOVING STARS

The Earth's spinning motion makes the stars seem to move across the night sky. The exception is the Pole Star, which seems to stay in the same place with the other stars revolving around it. The southern night sky has no Pole Star, and the area in the sky to which the Earth's South Pole points is almost empty of bright stars. The long axis of the famous Southern Cross (Crux) constellation in the southern sky points to the south celestial pole, the sky's south pole.

You are probably used to seeing a constellation, such as Orion, in the northern night sky. If you move closer to the Equator you will see the constellation on its side. As you move south, it will appear upside down and eventually disappear the farther south you travel. The same phenomena will happen to the southern stars as you travel north. The farther south you travel, the more of the southern sky you will see and the less of the north.

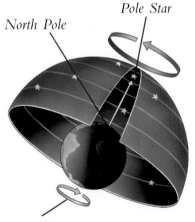

North Pole

Pole Star

Earth's rotation

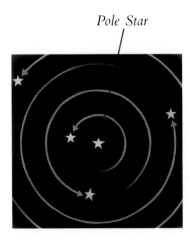

Pole Star

AT THE NORTH POLE
If you stood on the North Pole and looked up at the night sky, the Pole Star would be directly above your head. Because the Earth's axis points almost directly to the Pole Star, the other stars seem to revolve around it as the Earth rotates.

NORTH OF THE EQUATOR

If you stand on the Earth somewhere between 10 and 20 degrees north of the Equator, you will be in the mid-northern latitudes. The stars overhead will still seem to be moving, slowly changing the appearance of the sky from night to night.

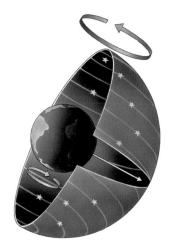

AT THE EQUATOR

An observer who stands at the Equator will see all the stars in the night sky during the period of a year. At the Equator, the stars seem to move in straight lines across the sky.

THE SOLAR SYSTEM

The Sun, together with the family of nine planets, comets, asteroids, and other bodies that travel round it, make up our Solar System. It was probably formed from a cloud of gas around 4.6 billion years ago. At the very heart of the Solar System lies the Sun, providing the heat and light that make life possible on the planet Earth.

Spacecrafts have visited all of the planets, with the exception of Pluto, the smallest and most distant planet. They have revealed a wealth of

different features on the planets,
including mountains and valleys, craters
and active volcanoes, colored ring systems,
poisonous atmospheres, and polar ice caps.
Earth is still the only planet in the Solar
System where we know that life definitely
exists, although scientists are continuously
looking for signs of life on all of the other
planets.

THE SUN AND FAMILY

Scientists believe that the Sun was born out of a cloud of hot gas and dust. As it started to become a fully fledged star, the remaining material was left orbiting the Sun at high speed. Specks of dust began to join together and form tiny rocks, which fused together gradually forming large bodies surrounded by clouds of gas. These bodies are the planets. The Solar System consists of nine known major planets: Mercury, Venus, Earth, Mars, Jupiter, Saturn, Uranus, Neptune, and Pluto.

Other material was left orbiting the Sun when the Solar System was formed. It includes the asteroids, a network of smaller minor planets most of which are orbiting the Sun between Mars and Jupiter. Other left-over material includes comets and small and large pieces of rock, called meteoroids, which travel in random orbits around the Sun.

THE EARTH IS FORMED

The Sun was formed out of a spinning cloud of gas and dust. The rest of the Solar System is thought to be made up of the remaining material left over after the formation of the Sun. The gas and dust attracted other material which slowly developed into the planets, including the Earth.

THE GAS PLANETS

Saturn is one of the four large gaseous planets in the Solar System. The others are Jupiter, Uranus, and Neptune. These large planets, which have small solid cores, are made mainly of frozen gas. Saturn's rings may consist of the original material left over when the Solar System was formed. Another, more likely theory is that the rings are the remains of a moon that came too close and then disintegrated under the forces of the planet's gravity. Jupiter, one of the other gas planets, is so large and has such a huge atmosphere that many astronomers believe it almost became a star.

SATURN , THE RINGED PLANET

The planet Saturn is considered to be the "star" of the Solar System. It has a well-formed system of rings and a number of moons. The other outer planets have much smaller ring systems.

HALLEY'S COMET

Comets are made of material left over when the planets were formed. They consist of dust and frozen gases. Comets shine in the sky because they are lit up by the Sun as they pass close to it.

35

THE SUN

 The Sun is 93 million miles (150 million km) away from the Earth. It is 109 times the size of the Earth and contains 99.9 percent of the mass of the whole Solar System. The Sun's center is like a huge nuclear furnace in which the temperature and pressure inside are so high that they set off atomic reactions. Here, atoms of hydrogen fuse together to form helium, and the energy produced at the core radiates out toward the surface.

The surface of the Sun is called the photosphere. The temperature here ranges from 7,740 degrees F (4,300 degrees C) to 16,200 degrees F (9,000 degrees C). The photosphere provides most of the light that comes from the Sun. The upper level of the photosphere, the chromosphere, is a stormy region of very hot gases. Here, the temperature has risen to nearly 2 million degrees F (1.1 million degrees C). The chromosphere is about 10,000 miles (16,000 km) thick. Above it, the Sun has a halo of even hotter gases called the corona.

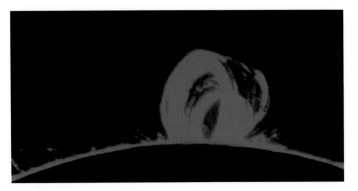

SOLAR ACTIVITY
Bright arches of hot glowing gas erupt from the surface of the Sun. These arches are called prominences. They may reach as far as 20 miles (30 km) above the Sun's surface. Some have a loop shape (above), while others are like a curtain of gas.

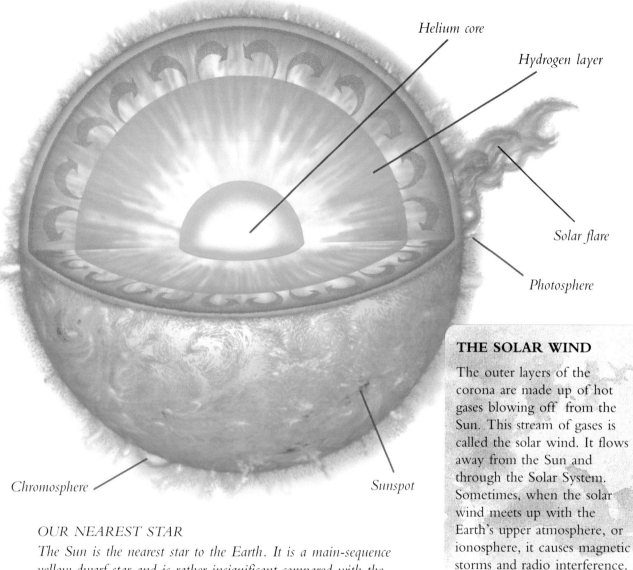

Helium core

Hydrogen layer

Solar flare

Photosphere

Chromosphere

Sunspot

OUR NEAREST STAR

The Sun is the nearest star to the Earth. It is a main-sequence yellow dwarf star and is rather insignificant compared with the much larger stars in the Milky Way. Light from the Sun takes 8 minutes, 17 seconds to reach the Earth, compared with the 4.3 light-years it takes to come from the next nearest star, Proxima Centauri. The center of the Sun is a huge nuclear furnace with a temperature of 27 million degrees F (15 million degrees C).

THE SOLAR WIND

The outer layers of the corona are made up of hot gases blowing off from the Sun. This stream of gases is called the solar wind. It flows away from the Sun and through the Solar System. Sometimes, when the solar wind meets up with the Earth's upper atmosphere, or ionosphere, it causes magnetic storms and radio interference. The solar wind also causes auroras, the red and green glowing lights that are visible in the night sky in the extreme parts of the northern and southern hemispheres.

MERCURY

Mercury, the nearest planet to the Sun, is a small rocky body with a diameter of 3,025 miles (4,880 km). The planet takes just 88 Earth days to travel once around the Sun at a distance of between 43 million miles (69 million km) and just 30 million miles (49 million km). The average distance of Mercury from the Sun is 35 million miles (57 million km), which is about half as close to the Sun as the Earth is.

The temperature in the intense sunlight on Mercury is hot enough to melt lead at midday. Mercury rotates very slowly, once every 58 Earth days. Because of this, each day on Mercury lasts 176 Earth days. The nighttime temperature is −320 degrees F(−180 degrees C). There is no atmosphere on Mercury and it would be impossible to live there.

MERCURY IN VIEW
Nobody knew what Mercury looked like until a space probe flew past the planet and took close-up pictures. Mercury looks very much like our own Moon. Its surface is covered with craters and mountains.

Because of its closeness to the Sun, Mercury never strays far from the Sun in the sky and so it is difficult to see. Occasionally, however, the small planet passes in front of the Sun as seen from Earth. This is called a transit. The next transit will occur on November 14, 1999. Observers who have the correct equipment to look safely at the Sun will see Mercury as a small, slow-moving dot.

A HOT, DRY PLANET

Mercury is a very hot, dry, and airless place. The planet is surrounded by a very thin layer of gases. Its surface is covered with many craters, which were probably formed when meteorites or comets crashed into the planet.

MERCURY FACT FILE

Diameter: 3,025 miles (4,880 km)

Average distance from Sun: 35.9 million miles (57.9 million km)

Length of a year: 88 Earth days

Number of moons: 0

VENUS

Venus is surrounded by thick clouds of carbon dioxide gas, which trap the Sun's heat, help to create a greenhouse effect on the planet. The trapped heat raises the temperature on the surface to 855 degrees F (475 degrees C), despite only about 2 percent of the Sun's light reaching the surface. The atmospheric pressure on Venus is 90 times greater than on Earth. Also, it rains sulfuric acid there. So if you stood on Venus, you would be boiled, squashed, and dissolved in one go! Venus is almost the same size as the Earth. It orbits the Sun at a distance of 67 million miles (108 million km) and takes 225 days to make one orbit, during which it sometimes comes within 25 million miles (40 million km) of the Earth. Because Venus rotates once every 243 days, a Venus day lasts 116 Earth days. Its thick clouds reflect the sunlight, making it one of the brightest objects in the sky.

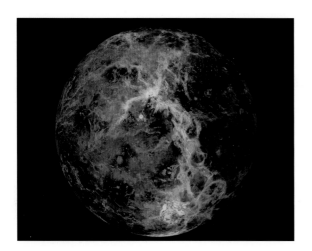

EARTH'S 'TWIN' PLANET
Venus is almost the same size as the Earth. It used to be known as Earth's sister or twin until people realized what was hidden beneath its thick sulphuric clouds. The surface of the planet is very hot and dry.

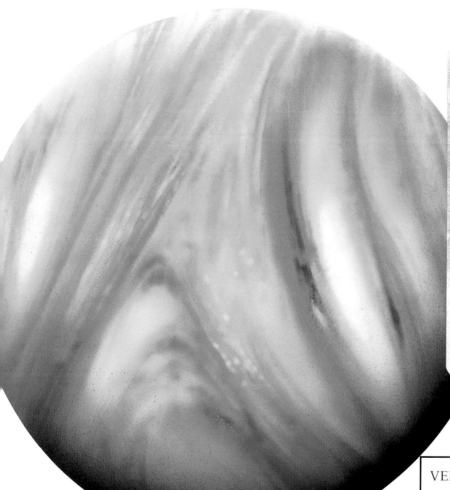

BRIGHT PLANET

The thick clouds that make up Venus's atmosphere reflect the sunlight brightly. It is therefore the brightest object in the Earth's skies apart from the Sun and the Moon. The planet's surface is covered with mountains, craters, and volcanoes, some of them bigger than Mount Everest, the highest mountain on the Earth.

VENUS FACT FILE

Diameter: 7,500 miles (12,100 km)

Average distance from Sun: 67.1 million miles (108.2 million km)

Length of a year: 225 Earth days

Number of moons: 0

41

THE EARTH

 The Earth orbits the Sun once every 365 days, or year. As it orbits the Sun, the Earth is rotating at a speed of 1,030 miles (1,660 km) per hour. It makes one rotation every 24 hours, or day. The Earth travels through space at a speed of almost 20 miles (30 km) per second, and in a year it travels a total distance of 595 million miles (960 million km).

The Earth has one moon which orbits at an average distance of 238,330 miles (384,400 km).

The Earth has an atmosphere that is rich in oxygen (21 percent) and nitrogen (78 percent). This atmosphere protects the Earth from deadly radiation from the Sun. About 70 percent of the Earth's surface is covered in liquid water in the form of the seas and oceans.

THE EARTH FROM SPACE
When seen from space, the Earth is the most beautiful and brightest planet. About three quarters of its surface are covered by very reflective oceans of water. If we could see the Earth from another planet, it would look like a bright bluish star.

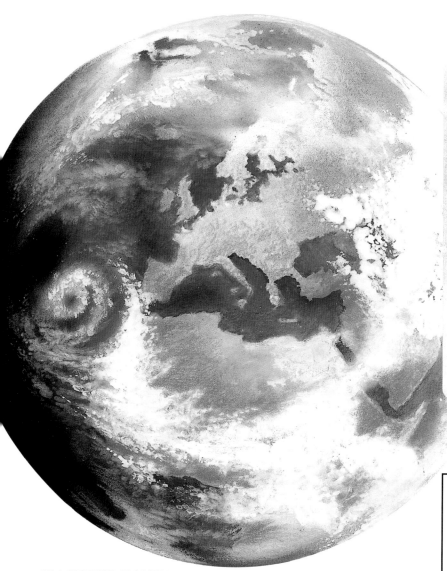

EARTH STATISTICS

• The temperatures on Earth vary from about – 128 degrees F (–89 degrees C) to about 136 degrees F (58 degrees C).

• The deepest point on the Earth is the Marianas Trench, which lies 35, 830 feet (10,924 m) below the Pacific Ocean.

• The highest point on the Earth is Mount Everest (29,021 feet/8,848 m).

•The North Pole does not point directly up because the Earth's axis is slightly tilted (by about 23.5 degrees).

EARTH FACT FILE

Diameter: 7,908 miles (12,756 km)

Average distance from Sun: 93 million miles (150 million km)

Length of a year: 365.25 Earth days

Number of moons: 1

SPACESHIP EARTH

The Earth is like a spaceship. It travels through space at a speed of almost 20 miles (30 km) per second. Although the Earth has a diameter of 7,908 miles (12,756 km), it has a very thin crust which is only 20 miles (32 km) thick.

OUR MOON

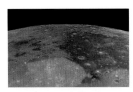

The Moon is about one third the size of the Earth. The Moon–Earth system is sometimes referred to as a "double planet." The Moon orbits the Earth every 27.5 days. Its surface is very dark because only about 7 percent of the Sun's light is reflected by it. The temperature on the Moon varies from 220 degrees F (105 degrees C) in the bright sunlight to minus –247 degrees F (–155 degrees C) in the shade. The pull of gravity on the Moon is only one-sixth of that on the Earth.

When you look at the Moon you can see the famous "Man in the Moon" face. This "face" is created by the lighter areas on the Moon's surface, which are covered by craters and mountains, and by the darker areas which are flat, wide plains. These

PHASES OF THE MOON
When the Moon is between the Sun and the Earth its far side is lit up, so we cannot see the side that faces us. When the Moon has moved farther round in its orbit we can see a crescent shape (far left), which gets bigger until a full Moon (center) appears.

plains were mistaken for "seas" by early astronomers, which explains why they have such names as Sea of Tranquillity.

INSIDE THE MOON
Scientists believe that the Moon's outer layer, or crust, is between 36 and 60 miles (60 and 100 km) thick. Beneath the crust is a thick layer of rock. The Moon's core is partly solid and partly liquid.

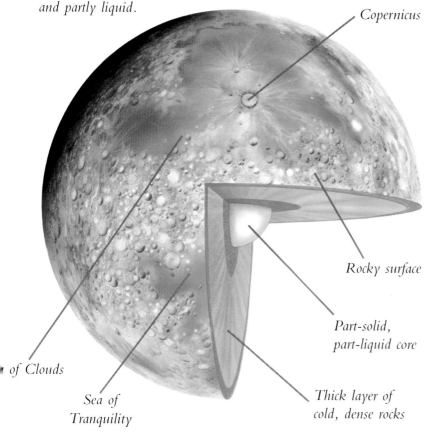

Copernicus

Rocky surface

Part-solid, part-liquid core

of Clouds

Sea of Tranquility

Thick layer of cold, dense rocks

MOON CRATERS
Many large craters on the Moon were named for famous people, especially famous astronomers. The most spectacular craters are those with "rays", which are made of material that was ejected from the craters when they were formed by the impact of meteorites. The most famous crater is called Tycho and can be seen clearly with the naked eye. The brightest crater is called Aristarchus. The largest crater on our side of the Moon is called Clavius. It has a diameter of 144 miles (232 km).

MOON FACT FILE

Diameter: 2,155 miles
3,476 km

Average distance from Earth: 238,328 miles (384,400 km)

Time taken to make a complete orbit of Earth: 27.5 Earth days

Average speed of orbit: 2,300 mph (3,700 km/h)

MARS

Mars has always excited astronomers because it is the only planet that can be observed clearly from Earth using quite small telescopes. Mars orbits the Sun every 687 days — the length of a Martian year. The length of a day on Mars is similar to that on Earth — 24 hours and 37 minutes.

Unlike the Earth, the atmosphere on Mars is 95 percent carbon dioxide. A maximum Martian temperature of −20 degrees F (−29 degrees C) makes Mars as cold as the coldest place on Earth. The atmospheric pressure there is just 1 percent that of the Earth's, so Mars would not be able to support life as we know it. Mars has two moons, called Deimos and Phobos. They are huge chunks of rock shaped like pockmarked potatoes. Phobos, the largest and closest one, is 17 miles (27 km) long and 12 miles (19 km) wide.

VIKING VISIT TO MARS
This image of the surface of Mars was taken by a Viking spacecraft that landed on the planet in 1976. The Martian surface is covered with reddish sand, dotted with various different sizes of rocks. The sand looks as though it may have been deposited by running water, which has also smoothed the rocks.

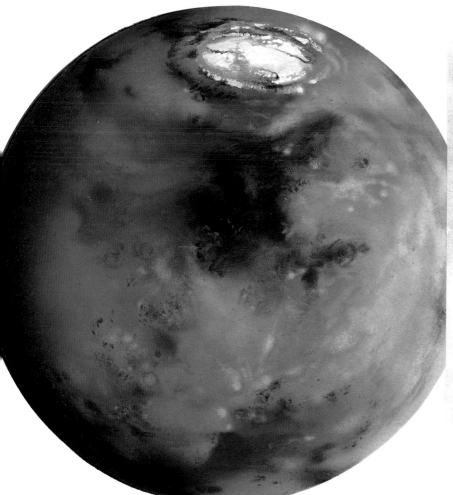

LIFE ON MARS

Early observations by telescope showed the dark areas on Mars changing shape during the year. The planet's polar ice caps were also sighted. People then started to think that water from the melting ice caps was helping to cultivate large areas of vegetation during the summer. One astronomer thought he could see lines on Mars, and the idea took off that there were Martians who had built irrigation canals! Mars then became the subject of many "sci-fi" stories, such as the famous H.G.Wells story *War of the Worlds*.

THE RED PLANET

Mars is sometimes called the Red Planet because it has a reddish surface, which indicates the presence of iron oxide in the soil. On the Earth, iron oxide is known as rust. Mars has a very active environment with dust storms, fog, frost, and polar ice caps made of dry carbon dioxide and water ice. Mars has a spectacular landscape of volcanoes, craters, and canyons.

MARS FACT FILE

Diameter: 4,208 miles (6,787 km)

Average distance from Sun: 141 million miles (227.9 million km)

Length of a year: 687 Earth days

Number of moons: 2

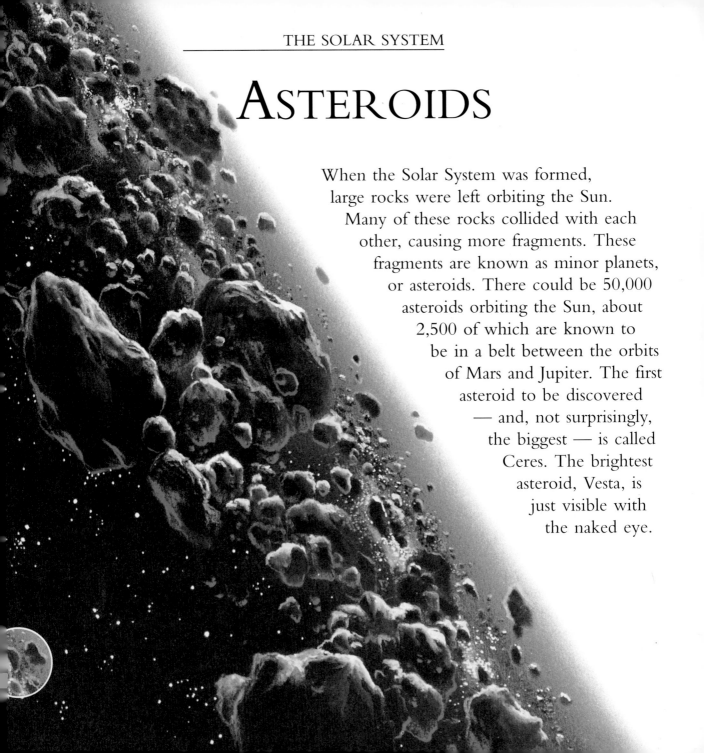

ASTEROIDS

When the Solar System was formed,
large rocks were left orbiting the Sun.
Many of these rocks collided with each
other, causing more fragments. These
fragments are known as minor planets,
or asteroids. There could be 50,000
asteroids orbiting the Sun, about
2,500 of which are known to
be in a belt between the orbits
of Mars and Jupiter. The first
asteroid to be discovered
— and, not surprisingly,
the biggest — is called
Ceres. The brightest
asteroid, Vesta, is
just visible with
the naked eye.

"SUN-GRAZERS"

The "Sun-grazer" Eros is an elongated asteroid. One of the most famous Sun-grazing asteroids is Icarus. It is just 0.9 miles (1.4 km) wide and comes to within 18 million miles (29 million km) of the Sun during its 1.1-year orbit. It actually glows red from the Sun's heat. In 1968, Icarus could be seen like a faint star traveling across the sky as it passed just 4 million miles (6.4 million km) from the Earth.

There are other asteroids in elliptical orbits around the Sun. These come close to the Earth in their orbits, then travel far out into the deepest parts of the Solar System. They are called "Sun-grazers". It is quite possible that asteroids have hit the Earth, causing extensive damage to its surface and the atmosphere. An asteroid impact might have been the cause of an explosion in 1908 in Siberia. It had a force equivalent to that of a 13-megaton nuclear bomb.

ROCKY BODIES

Thousands of asteroids orbit the Sun. These rocky bodies are the bits and pieces of material that seem to have been left over when the Solar System was formed. Although the largest asteroid is about 600 miles (1,000 km) wide, most of the known asteroids are less than 12 miles (20 km) in diameter.

JUPITER

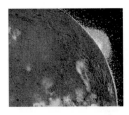

When the Solar System and the Sun were formed, Jupiter almost became another star. It is the largest planet, with a diameter of 88,540 miles (142,800 km). Jupiter is a huge ball of gases, including hydrogen, helium, ammonium, hydrogen sulfide and phosphorus. Bands of clouds of these gases swirl around Jupiter, which rotates quicker than any other planet — taking just 10 hours.

The colorful surface of Jupiter is dominated by the Great Red Spot, a swirling hurricane of gases where winds reach speeds of 21,700 miles per hour (35,000 km/h). The Great Red Spot could swallow up the Earth several times. Jupiter has at least 16 moons, and there could be many more that are too small to see. Its four major moons, from largest to smallest, are Ganymede, Callisto, Io, and Europa. Jupiter also has a small ring system that cannot be seen from Earth. It was discovered by a spacecraft sent to explore the giant planet.

Galilean moon

JUPITER FACT FILE

Diameter: 88,540 miles
(142,800 km)

Average distance from Sun:
482.5 million miles (778.3
million km)

Length of a year:
11.9 Earth years

Number of moons: 16

Faint rings made
of dust particles

Great Red Spot

THE LARGEST PLANET

Jupiter is the largest planet in the Solar System. Astronomers believe that it is a failed star which, had it been a bit bigger, could have helped to form a double-star system. Galileo made the first recorded observations of Jupiter through a telescope and saw four small specks orbiting the planet. These moved position each day. They are known as the Galilean moons.

JUPITER'S MOONS

The surface of Io is a dramatic world of orange, yellow and white deposits of sulfur and sulfur dioxide, with active volcanoes. Europa is like a huge ice pack, streaked with cracks. Underneath the ice pack there may be oceans of water, which some scientists think could be a source of basic living cells. Ganymede, the largest of the Galilean moons, has a surface that looks like a badly cracked eggshell, and Callisto has a pockmarked surface that resembles the skin of an avocado pear.

51

SATURN

 Saturn is the second largest planet in the Solar System. It takes 29.5 Earth years to make a complete orbit of the Sun. It was not long before early astronomers began to realize that Saturn is the most beautiful planet in the Solar System. Even early telescopes revealed a spectacular ring system. Saturn's rings are made up of thousands of "ringlets" small bits of rock and ice, all held together in an orbit by the planet's gravity.

Saturn also has at least 23 moons and may have many more. Some moons are within the ring system and are called "shepherd" moons, because they appear to help to keep the ring system in place. Saturn is like a smaller version of Jupiter, its atmosphere consisting mainly of hydrogen. Under the clouds, which rotate around the planet every 10 hours, are thick lakes of liquid hydrogen. The rocky core is 12,000 miles (20,000 km) wide.

A SYSTEM OF RINGS
Saturn's ring system is made up of billions of "snowballs" of rock and ice. They range in size from small flakes to chunks over 30 feet (9 m) wide.

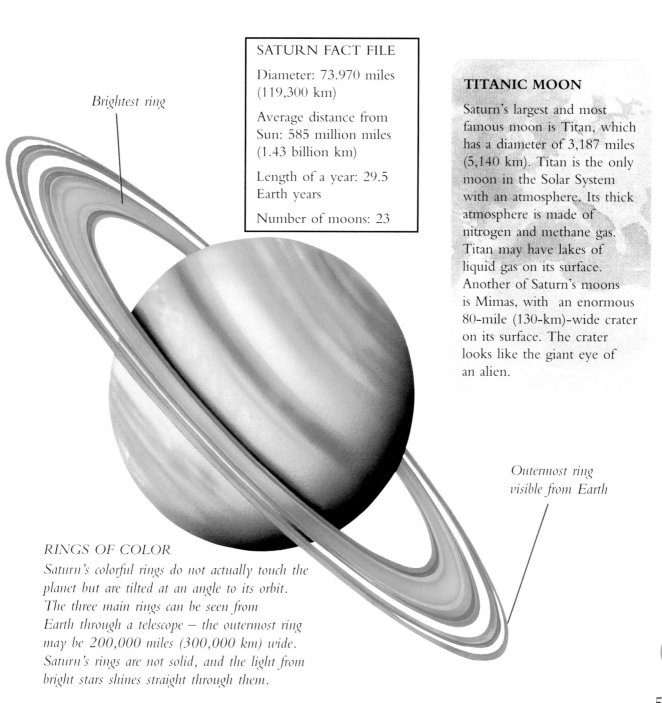

Brightest ring

TITANIC MOON

Saturn's largest and most
famous moon is Titan, which
has a diameter of 3,187 miles
(5,140 km). Titan is the only
moon in the Solar System
with an atmosphere. Its thick
atmosphere is made of
nitrogen and methane gas.
Titan may have lakes of
liquid gas on its surface.
Another of Saturn's moons
is Mimas, with an enormous
80-mile (130-km)-wide crater
on its surface. The crater
looks like the giant eye of
an alien.

*Outermost ring
visible from Earth*

RINGS OF COLOR

*Saturn's colorful rings do not actually touch the
planet but are tilted at an angle to its orbit.
The three main rings can be seen from
Earth through a telescope – the outermost ring
may be 200,000 miles (300,000 km) wide.
Saturn's rings are not solid, and the light from
bright stars shines straight through them.*

53

URANUS

Uranus was the first planet to be "discovered" — by English astronomer Sir William Herschel in 1781. It circles the Sun at an average distance from the Sun of 2 billion miles (2.87 billion km). The poles of this rather unusual planet point almost sideways, at an angle of 98 degrees. It is possible that Uranus was knocked over by a large body in the early history of the Solar System. Uranus is a bluish-green gas planet made up mainly of hydrogen and helium, with some methane. It has a very thin ring system of at least nine faint rings. The rings, which consist of rocks and dust, were only detected by astronomers in 1977. Uranus also has five large moons — Miranda, Ariel, Umbriel, Titania, and Oberon — as well as 10 small moonlets.

WILLIAM HERSCHEL
Uranus was the first planet to be "discovered" __ by William Herschel using a telescope in 1781, in Bath, England. All the other planets closer to the Sun can be seen with the naked eye.

A BLUE-GREEN PLANET

The methane gas in the atmosphere of Uranus gives the planet its bluish-green color. Methane gas accounts for about one-seventh of the atmosphere. Passing spacecrafts found streaks of cloud in the planet's upper atmosphere. Astronomers know very little about the surface of Uranus.

HERSCHEL'S DISCOVERY

Herschel made his discovery using a telescope in his garden in Bath, England. He compared the position of a star like object in the night sky against a star map and noticed that, during the following days, the object appeared to move in relation to the stars. He had discovered the seventh planet. Earlier astronomers had seen Uranus but had not noticed its slight movement in the sky.

NEPTUNE AND PLUTO

Neptune is a gaseous planet made of hydrogen and helium. It is very like Uranus but it is largely blue in color due to the composition of its atmosphere. Neptune has a very active atmosphere with high-speed winds that swirl around the planet faster than it rotates. The winds carry "scooter clouds" around the planet at speeds of 1,500 miles per hour (2,400 km/h). Neptune's orbit sometimes extends beyond the orbit of Pluto, as it did from 1979 to 1999. Neptune has two large moons, Triton and Nereid. Triton, one of the largest moons in the Solar System, is unusual because it moves in a circular orbit from east to west.

Pluto may well have been a moon of Neptune at one time. Its surface probably consists of frozen water, ammonia, and methane. Pluto is the most distant planet from the Sun. It takes 248 years to orbit the Sun and won't return to the position it was discovered in until 2177! It was discovered in 1930 by an American astronomer, Clyde Tombaugh.

NEPTUNE FACT FILE

Diameter: 30,690 miles
(49,500 km)

Average distance from Sun:
2.79 billion miles
(4.5 billion km)

Length of a year:
165 Earth years

Number of moons: 8

PLUTO FACT FILE

Diameter: 1,417 miles
(2,285 km)

Average distance from Sun:
3..65 billion miles
(5.9 billion km)

Length of a year:
248 Earth years

Number of moons: 1

PLANET DISCOVERIES

Astronomers predicted the existence of another planet beyond Uranus before it was finally discovered by a German, Johann Galle, in 1846. They had noticed that Uranus was not staying in a completely stable orbit around the Sun, and suspected that it was being pulled slightly off course by the gravity of another body. Mathematicians calculated where this possible planet might be, and Neptune was found in almost the exact spot predicted by Galle.

Pluto was discovered by Clyde Tombaugh after an extensive search which began at the Lowell Observatory, Arizona, USA. He compared photographic plates of the night sky and saw that a 'star' had moved.

THE DOUBLE PLANET

Pluto was the last planet to be discovered, and even the most powerful telescopes on Earth only show it as a star like point of light. Pluto's moon, Charon, was discovered in 1978. It is almost the same size as Pluto, and the Pluto–Charon system is rather like a double planet. Charon circles Pluto every 6.3 days. Because Pluto rotates every 6.3 days, Charon appears to be stationary in the sky, like a geostationary satellite orbiting the Earth.

COMETS

Head of comet

Comets are also made from material left over when the Solar System was formed. They are like "dirty snowballs" of rock, dust, and ice. They travel in various orbits around the Sun, usually going deep into the far reaches of the Solar System. The orbits of some comets bring them close to the Sun after many years in darkness. When they come near to the Sun, comets reflect the Sun's light and can be seen in our sky. The Sun's heat and light also make comets shed material, which normally forms into the characteristic long tail.

One of the most famous comets is Halley's Comet, which appears in our skies every 76 years. When it last came close to the Sun, in 1986, it was rather a disappointing sight. Recently, a much more spectacular comet was Hale–Bopp. It shone brightly in the night skies in 1996–1997, and had a spectacular double tail.

COMET KOHOUTEK
Comets are named after the people who discovered them. Lubos Kohoutek found a comet in 1970. It was observed from space by the Skylab 4 crew in early 1974.

COMETS IN ORBIT

As a comet approaches the Sun, the heat makes it expand, evaporating gas and releasing dust. The gas and dust form a fuzzy head and a long tail. About 400 comets take between 3 and 200 years to orbit the Sun. There are about 500 known comets that will not return to the region around the Sun for thousands of years.

HALLEY'S COMET

The first recorded sighting of Halley's Comet was in 86 BC. The comet appeared again in 1066, at the time of the Battle of Hastings. It can be seen on the famous Bayeux Tapestry. After another appearance in 1301, the Italian artist Giotto di Bondone depicted it in his famous painting, *The Adoration of the Magi*. It was named for Edmond Halley who, in the early eighteenth century, realized that sightings in 1682, 1607, and 1531 must have been of the same comet. He predicted its appearance in 1756, and the comet was named for him.

Tail of gas and dust

METEORITES

 Another kind of material left over from the formation of the Solar System consists of rocks of all shapes and sizes, and grain like particles of dust. These are meteoroids. They enter Earth's atmosphere at speeds of up to 30 miles (50 km) per second, burning up to leave behind a visible trail of hot gases called a meteor, or shooting star.

ARIZONA CRATER
A huge meteorite is thought to have hit the Earth in about 25,000 B.C. It created a huge crater 4,875 feet (1,265 m) wide and 574 feet (175 m) deep in Canyon Diablo, Arizona. The meteorite crashed with the force of a huge nuclear bomb.

METEORITE ROCK

*Some small meteoroids survive the heat
of entry into the Earth's atmosphere
and have been recovered. It is
possible to see about 10 meteors, or
shooting stars, an hour on a clear
night. During major periods of
meteor showers, more than 100
meteors an hour may be seen.*

Showers of
meteors tend to
occur during certain periods of the year.
For example, the Earth encounters dust from
Halley's Comet, which forms meteor showers
in May and October. As these appear in the part
of the sky where the constellations of Aquarius
and Orion are at the time, they are called the
Aquarids and the Orionids. Some of the larger
rocks, which cause the occasional spectacular
shooting star, survive the high-speed entry and
reach the Earth. These are called meteorites.
Several very large meteorites have hit the Earth
in its history, forming craters that we can still
see today.

METEORITE CLUES

About 500 meteorites hit the
Earth each year. The largest
known meteorite was found
at Grootfontein in Namibia,
southwest Africa, in 1920. It
is 9 feet (2.75 m) long and 8
feet (2.43 m) wide.
Recovered meteorites provide
scientists with an opportunity
to study some of the oldest
original material in the Solar
System. Grains of dust from a
meteorite that fell in
Murchison, Victoria, Australia
on September 28, 1969 are
thought to be older than the
Solar System itself.

INDEX

ACKNOWLEDGMENTS

The publishers wish to thank the following artists who have
contributed to this book.

Julian Baker, Kuo Kang Chen, Rob Jakeway, Darrell Warner
(Beehive Illustrations) Guy Smith, Janos Marffy,
Peter Sarson.

Photographs supplied by Genesis Photo Library and
Miles Kelly Archive.